LCM Exams

Anthology for Students of Drama and Communication

Introduction

This publication is primarily intended for candidates considering taking London College of Music examinations in Drama and Communication.

The anthology contains verse, prose and drama extracts for performance in Speech and Drama, Verse Speaking, Acting and Reading Aloud graded examinations and respective diplomas.

Examination candidates must also refer to the current LCM syllabus.

To enter for an examination, or for more details, please contact:

LCM Examinations
Thames Valley University
Walpole House
18-22 Bond Street
London W5 5AA

Tel: +44 (0)20 8231 2364

Fax: +44 (0)20 8231 2433

Email: lcm.exams@tvu.ac.uk
http://mercury.tvu.ac.uk/lcmexams

or your local representative

Published by:
LCM Publications
Thames Valley University
Walpole House
18-22 Bond Street
London W5 5AA

ISBN: 0 9528375 3 6

Compiled by Jocelyn Lord and Rex Satchwell

Typesetting by David Harvey

Contents

Notes

This book contains pieces which may be used for all levels of grade and diploma examinations. At each level, the pieces are presented in the following order: verse, prose and drama. In particular, a character name preceding a text denotes an acting piece.

Examination programmes should comply with the requirements set out in the syllabus. Dates (where known) have been provided at grade 6 and above to assist candidates in choosing pieces to fit these criteria.

Throughout the book, performance directions are given in curved brackets, and square brackets indicate material which is to be excluded in performance.

Foreword
by James Kirkup

Speak the Poet!

Good poetry anthologies are sometimes treasure-houses of the unexpected. Thematic anthologies that are collections of poems, old and new, on subjects like 'The Sea' or 'About Town' or 'Notes in Music' are usually very good, though appealing largely to the specialist on such universal themes. In complete contrast, there are what I call 'Ragbag' anthologies that are literary entertainments with a few unexpected new poems which stimulate a desire to read more work by some unknown poet.

The best anthologies are ones that serve some professional purpose, and the one now in your hands is one of them. It is full of excellent poems, all of them different in theme and tone of voice, what Shakespeare in *Hamlet* (Act III) calls 'poem unlimited' − 'pastoral-comical, historical-pastoral, tragical-historical'. . . etc. etc.

We say that variety is the spice of life − and that is why our poetic-dramatic appetites are whetted by a well-chosen selection of themes, poetic forms and styles. So there is a bit of something for everyone in this anthology − in which I am pleased to have the honour of being included. Do you ever think of the poor lonely poet scribbling away night and day and who unexpectedly chances upon one of his works in a new anthology? That is a radiant day for any poet, be he famous or unknown except for one poem 'that is in all the anthologies' as they say.

So when you practise a poem, you should imagine that you are the poet himself (or herself) just beginning to discover the first words, the first images, and then the final wonder of sound and sense that is a real, new poem! Even if the poem you choose is well-known and 'old as the hills', think of yourself as the poet slowly discovering the right words in the right place. And always wonder why he perhaps chose one unfamiliar word rather than a more usual one − it is that kind of linguistic surprise that helps to make a good poem, − and a good speaker of it! So go ahead and enjoy yourself − as we hope the poet did. But remember, he may have had to suffer almost unbearably to write the final version, that you are privileged to read aloud with all the ease and passion and joy that he (or she) did when the poem was finally completed. And remember that a poem can only exist − in writing and in your own voice − when it is completely absorbed by you − and when something of the poet's own voice speaks through you, his interpreter. You may sometimes actually feel you are a medium, transmitting the poet's message from beyond the grave.

STEP 1

THE LOST TABBY
by *Enid Barraclough*

I'm a shabby little Tabby
And I haven't any home –
Won't anybody take me in?
I'm a tired little Tabby
Ever on the roam,
I'm frightened of the noise and din.

I'm a shabby little Tabby
And I'm often very cold –
Won't somebody open a door?
I'm a lonely little Tabby
Tho' I'm not very old,
Will I never have a home any more?

SLUGS
by *John Kitching*

Slugs, slugs
Crawl through grass,
Watching all the beetles
As they scurry past.

Slugs, slugs
Crawl so slow,
Leaving tracks of silver
Wherever they go.

Slugs, slugs
Crawl along the wall.
Popping little horns out,
Make no sound at all.

THE WEED
by *Tricia Hawcroft*

I tried to grow a flower
I did what I was told
I kept it watered every day
And did not let it get cold.

Ten days passed and then I saw
A tiny little shoot,
I was so pleased because I knew
It must have had a root.

I felt so proud I'd grown this plant
From a little seed
But oh! How disappointing
When my mum said that's a weed.

THE MAN OUTSIDE
by *Richard Edwards*

There's a man in the street
And I don't like his stare
And I don't like the look
Of his prickly hair
And I don't like his size
Or his shape, he's too thin,
And I don't like his slouch
Or his lopsided grin,
But I'm not at all scared –
Do you want to know why?
It's November the fifth
And his name is Guy.

GLITTERBREAD
by *Brian Moses*

I'm so bored with pitta bread
I want glitterbread.

Bread that gleams when it catches the light,
bread that glows like the stars at night,

Bread that sparkles then starts to shimmer,
bread that dazzles and never grows dimmer,

Bread that lights my way back home,
bread that shines like a precious stone,

I want glitterbread all the time,
something new that's totally mine.

TEDDY BEAR
by *Tricia Hawcroft*

I wished I had a teddy bear
That I could call my own
Someone who would share with me
My thoughts when I'm alone.
He need not be a big one
And colour I don't mind,
Fat or thin, old or new
A bear of any kind.
I'd always keep him with me
Until the very end
For a teddy bear for some folks
Is always a best friend.

SNOW
by *Roy Fuller*

Snow falling in November
May fall on a yellow rose,
Forming an ice-cream cornet
That with ice-cream overflows.

When snow falls in December
It has only a bare black twig
To chalk on a sky of yellow
And make unusually big.

If snow should fall in April
How hard to tell its crumb
From petals cast in the border
Or blossom on the plum.

THE AIRMAN
Anon.

RRRRRRRRRRRR

The engine roars,
The propeller spins.
'Close the doors!'
Our flight begins.

ZZZZZZZZZZZZ

The plane rises;
It skims the trees.
Over the houses
We fly at our ease.

MMMMMM

ZOOM goes the plane,
The engine hums.
Then home again,
And down it comes...

MMMM
       M
        M
       M
MMMM
  Z
 Z
Z
 Z
  Z
    ZZZZZ RRRRRRRRRRRRRRRRRRRRRR

YES

by *Mary Ann Hoberman*

Yes
Yes
I like yes
I like it when I ask for things
And when you say yes
Yes
Yes
Let's take a walk
Let's bake a cake
Let's sing a song
Yes
Yes
And yet sometimes
I don't like yes
Like when you say
You've made a mess
Please clean it up
Or
Time for bed
Or
Time to go
And then I guess
That I like yes
A little less
Yes?
Yes.

BLACKBERRIES
by *Enid Barraclough*

There were blackberries in the hedges
Nestling in the green,
The ripest, blackest berries
I have ever seen.

Juicy little jewels gleaming with the dew –
The fruit was very tempting
So I gathered some for you.

There were blackberries in the hedges
Ripe and full and free,
So I filled a leaf with berries
And brought them for your tea.

RHAMPHORYNCHUS
(The flying reptile)
by *Wes Magee*

Look, as he swoops from the cliff's rugged face
  His squadrons of teeth instant death
To careless fish basking in shallow seas
  And lizards short of breath.

His tough skin is cracked and worn as old boots;
  His cries blood-curdle the night.
A Dracula beast with claws on his wings
  He glides . . . the world's first kite.

SNOW
by *Edward Thomas*

In the gloom of whiteness,
In the great silence of snow,
A child was sighing
And bitterly saying: 'Oh,
They have killed a white bird up there on her nest,
The down is fluttering from her breast!'
And still it fell through that dusky brightness
On the child crying for the bird of the snow.

MY PET MOUSE
by *Tricia Hawcroft*

When the clock struck one
I crept downstairs
I crept downstairs to see
My new pet mouse that Mummy bought,
She said, 'It looked like me.'

I find it hard to twitch my nose
And whiskers I have none
But in a year or maybe two,
I think that I'll grow some.

I haven't got two beady eyes,
My ears are both quite small
And standing by my mouse's side
I'm really very tall.

I don't think mummy sees so good,
I think she is a grouse
Cos I looked in the mirror
AND I DON'T LOOK LIKE A MOUSE!

MALICE AT BUCKINGHAM PALACE
by *Spike Milligan*

Outside Buckingham Palace
   a dog was barking one day
When out of a house
   came a chocolate mouse
And frightened that doggie away.

And so that chocolate mousie
   was taken to the Queen –
Who swallowed him up gobbledy slup
   with a gobbledy slup.
I do think that was mean.

THE LOO AT THE TOP OF THE STAIRS
by *Enid Barraclough*

I don't like the Loo at the top of the stairs,
It's white, and it looks like a ghost!
I know that it isn't, but that doesn't help –
It's the Loo that I'm frightened of most.

If someone forgets and leaves the door wide
I can see it up there in the gloom;
I think I'll be brave and go up the stairs
And pass by that dark little room.

I go up each step till I'm just half way
But that is the most I can do –
I make a dash down and wait in the Hall
Till the door is shut fast on the Loo!

CHAMELEON
by *Alan Brownjohn*

I can think sharply
and I can change:
my colours cover a reasonable range.

I can be some mud by
an estuary,
I can be a patch on the bark of a tree.

I can be green grass
or a little thin stone
– or if I really want to be left alone,

I can be a shadow. . . .
What I am on your
multi-coloured bedspread, I am not quite sure.

STEP 3

MOSQUITO
by *Peggy Dunstan*

At night
when I'm tucked tight in bed
you whine and dive
around my head.
You walk
  and stalk me
    up the sheet
with stick legs
bent up into feet.
There isn't any way you please
with elbows
where you should have knees –
and here's another horrid thing –
  you've got a sting.

THE DRAGON IN THE CELLAR
by *Nick Toczek*

There's a dragon!
There's a dragon!
There's a dragon in the cellar!
Yeah, we've got a cellar-dweller.
There's a dragon in the cellar.

He's a cleanliness fanatic,
takes his trousers and his jacket
to the dragon in the attic
who puts powder by the packet
in a pre-set automatic
with a rattle and a racket
that's disturbing and dramatic.

There's a dragon!
There's a dragon!
There's a dragon in the cellar
with a flame that's red 'n' yeller.
There's a dragon in the cellar. . .

DAFFODILS
by *Enid Barraclough*

I was walking –
I was walking
Inside a yellow wood,
I stopped and picked some Daffodils,
They grew just where I stood.

Then suddenly –
Then suddenly
I sat down on a stone,
I felt I was in Fairyland
And this my Fairy throne.

I tied my yellow Daffodils
Into a lovely bunch
To give them to the Fairy Queen
Before her royal lunch.

But then I felt so sleepy
I wandered home instead
And gave them to my Mummy
Before I went to bed.

SCHOOL

by *Tricia Hawcroft*

I had to learn my letters
And numbers too they said,
I had to get up early
But I wished I'd stayed in bed.

The other kids were noisy
And some of them were bad
The teacher shouted loud at us
We must have made her mad.

And once the day was over
I acted really cool
But now I know for certain
I really don't like school.

I have to go again it seems
And so I shed some tears
Mum smiled and said that I could leave
After about twelve years.

THE ALIEN

by *Julie Holder*

The alien
Was as round as the moon.
Five legs he had
And his ears played a tune.
His hair was pink
And his knees were green,
He was the funniest thing I'd seen
As he danced in the door
Of his strange spacecraft,
He looked at me –
And laughed and laughed!

THE SEA

by *Iain Crichton Smith*

Today the sea is playful and
casts a white froth across the sand
like the flounces on a long blue gown
which is shifting gently up and down.

Who would think that it would rage
like a great giant in a cage
swallowing sailor, ship and boat
and sucking them swiftly down its throat?

13

THE RAINMAKER DANCED
by *John Agard*

The rainmaker danced
the rainmaker danced
the rainmaker danced.

Down came
the rains
in a flash
and that was the end
of cricket match.

The rainmaker danced
the rainmaker danced
the rainmaker danced

Sky changed
from blue
to grey
and barbecue
was washed away

'What rotten luck!'
cried everyone, faces grim.
But what can you expect
when the rainmaker
was a magical duck
and dying for a swim.

I'M JUST GOING OUT
FOR A MOMENT
by *Mike Rosen*

I'm just going out for a moment.

Why?

To make a cup of tea.

Why?

Because I'm thirsty.

Why?

Because it's hot.

Why?

Because the sun's shining.

Why?

Because it's summer.

Why?

Because that's when it is.

Why?

Why don't you stop saying why?

Why?

DAYS
by *Brian Moses*

Days fly by on holidays
they escape like birds
released from cages.
What a shame you can't buy
tokens of time, save them up
and lengthen the good days,
or maybe you could tear out time
from days that drag, then pay it back on
holidays, wild days,
days you wish would last forever.
You could wear those days with pride,
fasten them like poppies to your coat,
or keep them in a tin like sweets,
a confection of days
to be held on the tongue
and tasted, now and then.

THE LEAVES IN A FROLIC
Anon.

The leaves had a wonderful frolic,
    They danced to the wind's loud song,
They whirled, and they floated, and scampered,
    They circled and flew along.

The moon saw the little leaves dancing,
    Each looked like a small brown bird.
The man in the moon smiled and listened,
    And this is the song he heard.

The North Wind is calling, is calling,
    And we must whirl round and round,
And when our dancing is ended
    We'll make a warm quilt for the ground.

MARCH SNOW
by *John Kitching*

It snows again today
And we go out to play
And sledge at the edge
Of the car-stuck road,
Wild and whirling,
Hurling snow cold and hard
From prickling hands,
Watching water trickling
From snow-crammed eaves,
Making an autumn of snowy leaves.
Graves in the churchyard
Lose their cold lead grey
And are warm in the white
Bitter cold that holds them
Gently free from ugly weeds
And decay for a day or two.

And I play with you
In this snow-time.

BORED
by *John Kitching*

I'm ten and I'm bored
And I've nothing to do.
I'm fed up with watching
This ant on my shoe.

The Big Game has finished.
My brother won't play.
My dad says he won't let me
Watch *Match of the Day*.

I don't want to paint
Or to make model planes
Or to help Mum with cooking
Or to stroll country lanes.

I'm bored with my school,
With my books on the shelf,
And, most of all really,
Bored with being myself.

NIGHT
by *Enid Barraclough*

Outside the sky is darkly blue,
The trees black shadows
Cast in silhouette –
Late birds twitter
Distant traffic hums,
The grass is shadowy now
No longer green.
The daffodils are standing
Sentinels –
Each one a yellow torch
Piercing the dark,
Till night time is complete
And all will sleep.
In these few moments
Swift the blackness comes –
Somewhere far away
The busy traffic hums.

THE STINK-A-BODS
by *Enid Barraclough*

The Stink-a-Bods are horrid things
That lurk in muddy weed-grown pools,
They make a nasty gurgling sound
When swimming in their murky schools.

I've never liked the Stink-a-Bods
And keep away from where they thrive,
The dirty, slimy, smelly ponds
With Stink-a-Bods they are alive.

So don't forget to watch your step
When out with fishing line or rod,
You'll do no good if you go near,
So please beware the Stink-a-Bod.

THE CONVERTIBLES
by *Stanley Cook*

Those baskets on wheels in the superstore
That turn on a fivepence
And glide on rubber-tyred, ballbearinged wheels
Along the floor
Would be perfect partners for a dance
Up the middle of biscuits and cereals
And round the salad stall
Past the checkpoint
And out at the door.

Or the same base
With a streamlined body
Would make a stainless steel
Soapbox racer.

Can't you see
A touring Eskimo
Filling it with a load
Of frozen food,
Harnessing his team
And mushing down the road?

So many things
Apart from carrying
The family shopping
That baskets on wheels
Could be useful for.

THE BROKEN TOYS
by *James Kirkup*

In the broken box
The broken toys –
    Dusty,
Battered and rusty,
Tattered and torn,
        Forlorn, forlorn.

The snapped strings
And the busted springs,
The rag-doll raggy and rent,
The pink tin teaset buckled and bent,
        The crashed plane,
        The car, the train –
Smashed in a terrible accident.

And all the dolls' eyes
Rolling loose like heavy marbles
Up the dolls' house stairs and down
The stairs of the overturned house . . .
The dead wheels of a clockwork mouse.

In the broken box
The broken toys –
        .Dusty,
Battered and rusty,
Tattered and torn,
        Forlorn, forlorn.

from A BEAR CALLED PADDINGTON

by *Michael Bond*

Paddington eyed the tray hungrily. There was half a grapefruit in the bowl, a plate of bacon and eggs, some toast, and a whole pot of marmalade, not to mention a large cup of tea. 'Is all that for me?' he exclaimed.

'If you don't want it I can soon take it away again,' said Mrs Bird.

'Oh, I do,' said Paddington hurriedly. 'It's just that I've never seen so much breakfast before.'

'Well, you'd better hurry up with it.' Mrs Bird turned in the doorway and looked back. 'Because you're going on a shopping expedition this morning with Mrs Brown and Judy. And all I can say is, thank goodness I'm not going too!' She closed the door.

'Now I wonder what she means by that?' said Paddington. But he didn't worry about it for very long. There was far too much to do. It was the first time he had ever had breakfast in bed and he soon found it wasn't quite so easy as it looked. First of all he had trouble with the grapefruit. Every time he pressed it with his spoon a long stream of juice shot up and hit him in the eye, which was very painful. And all the time he was worried because the bacon and eggs were getting cold. Then there was the question of the marmalade. He wanted to leave room for the marmalade.

In the end he decided it would be much nicer if he mixed everything up on the one plate and sat on the tray to eat it.

from THE BFG

by *Roald Dahl*

'Do we really have to eat it?' Sophie said.

'You do unless you is wanting to become so thin you will be disappearing into a thick ear.'

'Into *thin air*,' Sophie said. 'A thick ear is something quite different.'

Once again that sad winsome look came into the BFG's eyes. 'Words,' he said, 'is oh such a twitch-tickling problem to me all my life. So you must simply try to be patient and stop squibbling. As I am telling you before, I know exactly what words I am trying to say, but somehow or other they is always getting squiff-squiddled around.'

'That happens to everyone,' Sophie said.

'Not like it happens to me,' the BFG said. 'I is speaking the most terrible wigglish.'

'I think you speak beautifully,' Sophie said.

'You do?' cried the BFG, suddenly brightening. 'You really do?'

'Simply beautifully,' Sophie repeated.

from THE WITCHES

by *Roald Dahl*

Mr Jenkins had not gone more than a few paces towards The Grand High Witch's table when a piercing scream rose high above all the other noises in the room, and at the same moment I saw The Grand High Witch go shooting up into the air!

Now she was standing on her chair, still screaming. . .

Now she was on the table-top, waving her arms. . .

'What on earth's happening, Grandmamma?'

'Wait!' my grandmother said. 'Keep quiet and watch.'

Suddenly all the other witches, more than eighty of them, were beginning to scream and jump up out of their seats as though spikes were being stuck into their bottoms. Some were standing on chairs, some were up on the tables and all of them were wiggling about and waving their arms in the most extraordinary manner.

Then, all at once, they became quiet.

Then they stiffened. Every single witch stood there as stiff and silent as a corpse.

The whole room became deathly still.

'They're shrinking, Grandmamma!' I said.

from MARY POPPINS COMES BACK

by *P. L. Travers*

Mary Poppins bent down and opened the carpet-bag. It was quite empty except for a large thermometer.

'What's that for?' asked Jane curiously.

'You!' said Mary Poppins.

'But I'm not ill!' Jane protested. 'It's two months since I had measles.'

'Open!' said Mary Poppins, in a voice that made Jane shut her eyes very quickly and open her mouth. The thermometer slipped in.

'I want to know how you've been behaving since I went away!' remarked Mary Poppins sternly.

Then she took out the thermometer and held it up to the light.

'Careless, Thoughtless and Untidy,' she read out.

Jane stared.

'I'm not surprised!' said Mary Poppins, and thrust the thermometer into Michael's mouth. He kept his lips tightly pressed upon it until she plucked it out and read:

'A very Noisy, Mischievous, Troublesome little Boy.'

'I'm not,' he said angrily.

For answer she thrust the thermometer under his nose and he spelt out the large red letters.

'A-V-E-R-Y-N-O-I-S...'

'You see?' said Mary Poppins, looking at him triumphantly. She opened John's mouth and popped in the thermometer.

'Peevish and Excitable.' That was John's temperature.

And, when Barbara's was taken, Mary Poppins read out the two words, 'Thoroughly Spoilt.'

'Humph!' she snorted. 'It's about time I came back!'

from WILLIAM AND THE POP SINGERS

by *Richmal Crompton*

WILLIAM: Well, the story starts in South Africa – that's where they find diamonds, you know – an' one of this gang goes over there an' fills the tyres of his car solid with diamonds. Then he drives it back an' takes it across the channel in a ferry disguised as a fishin' boat, then he drives it to this golf club here an' puts it in the garage. Then, in the dead of night, they take the diamonds out of the tyres an' put 'em into golf balls. Then the nex' day they pretend to play golf an' play with these balls an' keep losin' them in the long grass, but they know jus' where they are really an' next night someone goes round puttin' them into sacks an' fillin' up the tops of the sacks with potatoes, an' loads them on to lorries an' takes them up to Covent Garden and there's more of the gang at Covent Garden disguised as greengrocers an' they take these sacks an' put them in their cars an' take 'em off to diamond fences.

['What's that?' said Ginger.]

Gosh, don't you know what a fence is? It's a person that buys stolen stuff an' a diamond fence is a person that buys smuggled diamonds. This gang makes *pounds* of money that way. They're *rollin'* in money. Why, look at Lieutenant-Colonel Pomeroy havin' that swimmin' pool made in his garden. My mother said it mus' have cost the earth. Well, that *proves* it, doesn't it?

from THE SNOW QUEEN

by *Suria Magito and Rudolf Weil*

Kay is revealed seated on the ice throne of the Snow Queen. He is rigid except for his lips, which are moving.

(Suddenly the weird music announcing the approach of the Snow Queen sounds again. She enters.)

SNOW QUEEN: (*smiling*) Are you still thinking about your figures? Think about them while I am gone, Kay.

Yes, I must leave you all alone in my palace. But only for a very short time. I shall fly on my black cloud far, far away to the warm south, to sprinkle the mountain-tops with snow.

How clever you are. With your brain and your heart of ice. . . (*Suddenly with anxiety:*) Do you feel cold? I must kiss you again so that your heart does not melt while I am away. (*She kisses him and he freezes still more.*) You are mine, for ever and always!

(*to herself:*) No one shall take you from me. . . . My polar bears and my ice birds guard the door – and even if any creatures passed them, they would never find their way to you, through all the thousand empty icy halls of my palace. . . . (*Then aloud again.*) Now, polar wind, come and cut through these icy walls. . . and carry me away – to the south!

(*She begins to dance, generating the speed of the north wind – then she sweeps through the walls. The music ends abruptly.*)

WHO?

by *Wes Magee*

'Who,' asked my mother,
'helped themselves to the *new* loaf?'
  My two friends and I
  looked at her
  and shrugged.

'Who,' questioned my mother,
'broke off the crust?'
  Three pairs of eyes
  stared at the loaf
  lying on the kitchen table.

'Who,' demanded my mother,
'ate the bread?'
  No one replied.
  You could hear
  the kitchen clock. Tick. Tock.

And
even now I can taste it,
crisp, fresh, warm from the bakery,
  and I'd eat it again
  if I could find a loaf
  like that, like that...

AWAY GO WE

by *Walter de la Mare*

One, two, three,
And away go we!
Shingle, starfish,
Sand, and sea!
Wind on cheek,
Clear sun on skin;
The tumbling waves
Sweep out, sweep in.

A magic, broken
Music calls
In the water
As it falls;
Voices, a sigh,
A long-drawn *hush*,
As back – in myriad
Bubbles – gush
The green-grey ripples,
Flecked with snow –
A music solemn,
Sweet, and low.

SQUIRRELS

by *Enid Barraclough*

Be quiet!   A squirrel
Is nibbling under the tree!
A Tree-Rat you say?
Ah yes, but he
Is nibbling, nibbling,
Doing no harm
To you or me.

Hush!   No sound!
Another Squirrel
Comes with a bound
And like the other
He nibbles under the tree
Doing no harm
To you or me.

Oh see!   The furry pair
Two grey squirrels
Feed over there.
Both have fine
Big bushy tails,
Nibbling under the tree
Doing no harm
To you or me.

WINTER MORNING
by *Ogden Nash*

Winter is the king of showmen,
Turning tree stumps into snow men
And houses into birthday cakes
And spreading sugar over lakes.
Smooth and clean and frosty white,
The world looks good enough to bite.
That's the season to be young,
Catching snowflakes on your tongue.

Snow is snowy when it's snowing,
I'm sorry it's slushy when it's going.

THE LOVE-DOOMED RAT
by *Brian Patten*

O poor rat! Poor rat!
It fell in love with a cat! A cat!

O what will become of it!
It's hated enough for spreading plague and stuff,
it's hated enough!

It lived underground without the sun,
in its drab-dark world it had no fun.

Poor rat!
The trouble it's taken to make itself clean!
So love-starved and so lean!

It says:
'My eyes are tiny and hers like the moon,
and soon, O soon I must risk it –
I must visit that cat's basket!'

O what will become of it,
Struck by love to such a weird degree,
as love-sick as you or I could be.

BRAVADO
by *Enid Barraclough*

Who says I'm afraid because it's dark?
There's nothing out there in the hall –
There's only a clock going tickety-tock,
I'm really not frightened at all.

Who says I'm scared when the lights are out?
I don't mind the shadows outside;
It's easy to see it's only a tree
So there's really no need to hide.

Who says I'm frightened of something queer
That's crouching right under my bed?
There's nothing there, so why should I scare –
And why should I bother my head?

Afraid of the dark? Of course I'm not,
And of course my heart doesn't knock –
For why should I fear when all I can hear
Is that friendly old tickety-tock.

HUGGER MUGGER
by *Kit Wright*

I'd sooner be
Jumped and thumped and dumped,

I'd sooner be
Slugged and mugged . . . than *hugged* . . .

And clobbered with a slobbering
Kiss by my Auntie Jean:

You know what I mean:

Whenever she comes to stay,
You know you're bound
To get one.
A quick
  short
  peck
  would
  be
  OK
But this is a
Whacking great
Smacking great
  Wet one!

IN THE PLAYGROUND
by *Michael Rosen*

In the playground
at the back of our house
there have been some changes:

They said:
the climbing frame's not safe
So they sawed it down.

They said:
the paddling pool's not safe
so they drained it dry.

They said:
The see-saw's not safe
so they took it away.

They said:
the sand pit's not safe
so they fenced it in.

They said:
the playground's not safe
so they locked it up.

sawn down
drained dry
taken away
fenced in
locked up.

How do you feel?
Safe?

from GEORGE'S MARVELLOUS MEDICINE

by *Roald Dahl*

'Where's that medicine of mine, boy?!' came the voice from the living room. 'You're forgetting me! You're doing it on purpose! I shall tell your mother!'

'I'm not forgetting you, Grandma', George called back. 'I'm thinking of you all the time. But there are still ten minutes to go.'

'You're a nasty little maggot!' the voice screeched back. 'You're a lazy and disobedient little worm, and you're growing too fast.'

George fetched the bottle of Grandma's real medicine from the sideboard. He took out the cork and tipped it all down the sink. He then filled the bottle with his own magic mixture by dipping a small jug into the saucepan and using it as a pourer. He replaced the cork.

Had it cooled down enough yet? Not quite. He held the bottle under the cold tap for a couple of minutes. The label came off in the wet but that didn't matter. He dried the bottle with a dishcloth.

All was now ready!

This was it!

The great moment had arrived!

'Medicine time, Grandma!' he called out.

from ANNE OF GREEN GABLES

by *L. M. Montgomery*

Christmas morning broke on a beautiful white world. It had been a very mild December and people had looked forward to a green Christmas; but just enough snow fell softly in the night to transfigure Avonlea. Anne peeped out from her frosted gable window with delighted eyes. The firs in the Haunted Wood were all feathery and wonderful; the birches and wild cherry-trees were outlined in pearl; the ploughed fields were stretches of snowy dimples; and there was a crisp tang in the air that was glorious. Anne ran downstairs singing until her voice re-echoed through Green Gables.

'Merry Christmas, Marilla! Merry Christmas, Matthew! Isn't it a lovely Christmas? I'm so glad it's white. Any other kind of Christmas doesn't seem real, does it? I don't like green Christmasses. They're *not* green – they're just nasty faded browns and greys. What makes people call them green? Why – why – Matthew, is that for me? Oh, Matthew!'

from CHILDREN ON THE OREGON TRAIL

by *A. Rutgers van der Loeff*

He had reached the top. He made his last steps slowly, very slowly. He looked down over the other side. He saw. . .

That . . . that was impossible! How could it be, so – so suddenly? It was such a wonderful sight, what he saw there. So splendid, so unbelievable, so . . . it must be an optical illusion, he thought. He shook his head and shut his eyes. Then he opened them again. He looked at Indepentia, he looked down . . . it was *not* an optical illusion, it was what he had been hungering for all those weeks, and now that it was there he could not believe it.

Far below him, far below this last chain of the Blue Mountains, lay a wide, long, green valley, with trees and shrubs still clad in their autumn yellow. There were the small square shapes of a few log cabins, a thin plume of smoke rose from a chimney – it was the mission station of Dr Marcus Whitman. It was Oregon; it must be the Columbia valley. Down there he saw a winding, silver ribbon with edges of luxurious green.

Great Father in Heaven, they were there!

He did not look round at the others. He did not beckon and he did not wave; he did not shout. He stood motionless, gazing down, and let them come.

from DOUBLE ACT

by *Jacqueline Wilson*

If our writing's a bit shaky, it's because we're doing this account in the van.

We feel shaky. Our whole lives have been shaken up.

Dad really has bought a bookshop! He didn't even take us with him to check it out first. He went away for the weekend with Rose, and when he came back he said, 'Guess what! I've bought a shop.'

We just stared at him, stunned. He's been acting so crazy. Not like a dad at all. Especially not our dad.

We're used to him saying, 'Guess what! I've bought another box of books.'

But you don't buy a book*shop* just like that. You're meant to hang around for months, getting it surveyed and seeing solicitors.

'It's all simple,' said Dad. 'This sweet old couple are retiring and are happy to move out straight away. If I can't sell our own house, I'll let it out to students for a bit. Your gran's got her sheltered flat all worked out. Rose only rents her room, and she can shut up her stall in the arcade any time, so she hasn't got any problems either.'

We're the ones with the problems. Garnet and me.

from TOAD OF TOAD HALL

by *A. A. Milne*

JUDGE: Of course he's guilty. That isn't the point. The only difficulty which presents itself in this otherwise very clear case is, how can we possibly make it sufficiently hot for the incorrigible rogue and hardened ruffian whom we see cowering in the Dock before us? Mr Usher, will you please tell us what is the very stiffest penalty we can impose for each of the three offences for which the prisoner stands convicted? Without, of course, giving him the benefit of the doubt, because there isn't any. . .

Silence! An excellent suggestion, Mr Usher. Now, prisoner, pull yourself together and try and stand up straight. It's going to be twenty years for you this time. And mind, if you appear before us again, on any charge whatever, we shall have to deal with you very seriously. . .

Twenty years. Don't forget. Now then, prisoner, before the rest of us adjourn for lunch, is there anything you would like to say in the nature of a farewell speech? Any last words or valedictory utterances?

(*aghast*:) Fat-face? ME? Well, of all the ungrateful things to say! To call *me*, after all I've done for him, fat-face! . . .

Silence! Stop him somebody! Stop him! Take him away! Cast him into the dungeon! Load him with chains! Gag him!

from THE SNOW QUEEN

by *Suria Magito and Rudolf Weil*

STORYTELLER: At that time my mother – just like Granny – went out to work for other ladies all day. But she wasn't so strong as Granny and like me her hands were clumsy; so it would often occur that she didn't get home till very late. Now one evening I was waiting patiently. It was later than she'd ever been and it was winter. The wind was blowing like – well, like tonight . . . a North wind. Well, I waited and I waited, but presently the candle burnt right down and went out. Then I got frightened. The old street lamp outside our window creaked and swung about in the wind; and as it swung to and fro it sent weird shadows scampering across the floor and up and down the walls of the room. I snatched my cap and scarf and ran out of the house, slamming the door. It wasn't so eerie waiting out in the street. It was dead quiet. I pushed aside some dry snow and sat on the step. Then – suddenly – the wind whipped dry snow off the street, and the roofs and the railings and the gate. And it all whirled round and round in the wind till I could hardly see it for snow. *Then it happened* ——— Inside the whirling snow a very beautiful white shape grew, like the hugest snowflake you ever saw, and as the wind blew faster and snowflakes flew around and around it grew and grew and grew and grew till . . .

(*A great gust of wind and at the same time his hand sweeps the lamp off the table and there is a blackout.*)

It was my clumsy hands again! I'll light the lamp.

GRADE 3

HIGH

by *Walter de la Mare*

Fly, kite!
High!
Till you touch the sky!
Stoop, whistling in the wind;
And whisper down the quivering string
If, as you soar, you find
The world we tread is like a ball –
With mounds for hills, and ponds for seas,
Its oxen small as creeping bees,
Mere bushes its huge trees!

But ah, the dew begins to fall,
The evening star to shine,
Down you must sink to earth again –
An earth, I mean, like mine.

THE LONELY SCARECROW

by *James Kirkup*

My poor old bones – I've only two –
A broomshank and a broken stave,
My ragged gloves are a disgrace,
My one peg-foot is in the grave.
I wear the labourer's old clothes;
Coat, shirt and trousers all undone.
I bear my cross upon a hill
In rain and shine, in snow and sun.
I cannot help the way I look.
My funny hat is full of hay.
– O, wild birds come and nest in me!
Why do you always fly away?

THE NEWCOMER
by *Brian Patten*

'There's something new in the river,'
The fish said as it swam –
'It's got no scales, no fins and no gills,
And ignores the impassable dam.'

'There's something new in the trees,'
I heard a bloated thrush sing,
'It's got no beak, no claws and no feathers,
And not even the ghost of a wing.'

'There's something new in the warren,'
Said the rabbit to the doe.
'It's got no fur, no eyes and no paws,
Yet digs deeper than we dare go.'

'There's something new in the whiteness,'
Said the snow-bright polar bear.
'I saw its shadow on a glacier,
But it left no pawmarks there.'

Through the animal kingdom
the news was spreading fast –
No beak, no claws, no feather,
No scales, no fur, no gills,
It lives in the trees and the water,
In the soil and the snow and the hills.
And it kills and it kills and it kills.

THE PERFORMING BAG
by *Stanley Cook*

The plastic bag that once was full
Of coloured sweets was empty and lost
And lay against the playground wall,
Flat and still among the dust.

But a wind came up the road,
Brushing back the hair of the grass,
Trying to unbutton people's coats
And teasing the leaves as it passed.

It felt its way inside the bag
Like a hand inside a glove
And like a puppet waking up
The plastic bag began to move.

As the air inside it puffed it out,
The bag that was lying sad and flat
Began to waggle its corners about
And nodded its head this way and that.

It dodged its way between the children
Who watched it carried high in the sky,
And disappear on the hand of the wind
Waving them goodbye.

WHICH

by *Leonard Clark*

Would you rather be

Thin

as

a

Pin

or

Lean

as

a

Sardine?

Or do you agree

It would be better if you were as Thick as an old oak Tree,

Fat as a pig, or harvest pumpkin, or dusty honey bee?

O dear me, no

I don't want to become

Tiny like Tom Thumb

or grow

Small enough to live with a mouse

in his house;

I don't want to be as Big as an elephant, Wider than a bus,

Huge as a fairy tale giant or a hippopotamus,

I think I'd rather stay

Just as I am if I may,

The same size tomorrow as yesterday.

NOT GUILTY
by *John Kitching*

We have assembly every day
Assembly in the hall
And every day (or so it seems)
The Head, who's ten feet tall
(Or so it seems) has lots to say
About the writing on the wall.
And (so it seems) just every day
He looks at me with marbled eye
And makes me feel I wrote it all.
I go quite red from head to foot
(Or so it seems) and try to stare
Right back at him.
            'How do you dare,'
I want to shout, 'to make me feel
I wrote that stuff?' I'm more the type
Who'd look for rags to wipe
It out (or so it seems.)

THE MOLE
by *Stanley Cook*

Tube-dweller, he travels at speed
The main lines of the underground
Or starts branch lines beneath the fields,
Domed above by the earth he shovels out.

Dressed for the underground dirt and wet,
He lives in a twenty-four hour night
And could hardly tell the difference
Between darkness and light.

The whole of his life is spent in escaping
In tunnels he digs with his own two hands;
When the owl and the weasel hunt above ground,
The tunnels themselves mean freedom to him.

CHRISTMAS DAY
by *Roy Fuller*

Small girls on trikes
Bigger on bikes
Collars on tykes

Looking like cads
Patterned in plaids
Scarf-wearing dads

Chewing a choc
Mum in a frock
Watches the clock

Knocking in pans
Fetching of grans
Gathering of clans

Hissing from tins
Sherries and gins
Upping of chins

Corks making pops
'Just a few drops'
Watering of chops

All this odd joy
Tears at a broken toy
Just for the birth long ago of a boy

from THE SECRET GARDEN

by *Frances Hodgson Burnett*

One marvel of a day he had walked so far that when he returned the moon was high and full and all the world was purple shadow and silver. The stillness of lake and shore and wood was so wonderful that he did not go into the villa he lived in. He walked down to a little bowered terrace at the water's edge and sat upon a seat and breathed in all the heavenly scents of the night. He felt the strange calmness stealing over him and it grew deeper and deeper until he fell asleep.

He did not know when he fell asleep and when he began to dream; his dream was so real that he did not feel as if he were dreaming. He remembered afterwards how intensely wide awake and alert he had thought he was. He thought that as he sat and breathed in the scent of the late roses and listened to the lapping of the water at his feet, he heard a voice calling. It was sweet and clear and happy and far away. It seemed very far, but he heard it as distinctly as if it had been at his very side.

'Archie! Archie! Archie!' it said, and then again, sweeter and clearer than before 'Archie! Archie!'

He thought he sprang to his feet not even startled.

It was such a real voice and it seemed so natural that he should hear it.

'Lilias! Lilias!' he answered. 'Lilias! where are you?'

'In the garden,' it came back like a sound from a golden flute. 'In the garden!'

And then the dream ended. But he did not awaken. He slept soundly and sweetly all through the lovely night. When he did awake at last it was brilliant morning and a servant was standing staring at him.

from OLIVER TWIST

by *Charles Dickens*

It was market morning. The ground was covered, nearly ankle-deep, with filth and mire; a thick steam, perpetually rising from the reeking bodies of the cattle, and mingling with the fog, which seemed to rest upon the chimney-tops, hung heavily above. All the pens in the centre of the large area, and as many temporary pens as could be crowded into the vacant space, were filled with sheep; tied up to posts by the gutter side were long lines of beasts and oxen, three or four deep. Countrymen, butchers, drovers, hawkers, boys, thieves, idlers, and vagabonds of every low grade, were mingled together in a mass; the whistling of drovers, the barking of dogs, the bellowing and plunging of oxen, the bleating of sheep, the grunting and squeaking of pigs; the cries of hawkers, the shouts, oaths, and quarrelling on all sides; the ringing of bells and roar of voices, that issued from every public-house; the crowding, pushing, driving, beating, whooping and yelling; the hideous and discordant din that resounded from every corner of the market; and the unwashed, unshaven, squalid, and dirty figures constantly running to and fro, and bursting in and out of the throng, rendering it a stunning and bewildering scene, which quite confounded the senses.

Mr Sikes, dragging Oliver after him, elbowed his way through the thickest of the crowd, and bestowed very little attention on the numerous sights and sounds, which so astonished the boy.

from FIVE CHILDREN AND IT

by *E. Nesbitt*

Then Anthea cried out, '*I'm* not afraid. Let me dig,' and fell on her knees and began to scratch like a dog does when he has suddenly remembered where it was that he buried his bone.

'Oh, I felt fur,' she cried, half laughing and half crying. 'I did indeed! I did!' when suddenly a dry husky voice in the sand made them all jump back, and their hearts jumped nearly as fast as they did.

'Let me alone,' it said. And now everyone heard the voice and looked at the others to see if they had too.

'But we want to see you,' said Robert bravely.

'I wish you'd come out,' said Anthea, also taking courage.

'Oh, well – if that's your wish,' the voice said, and the sand stirred and spun and scattered, and something brown and furry and fat came rolling out into the hole and the sand fell off it, and it sat there yawning and rubbing the ends of its eyes with its hands.

'I believe I must have dropped asleep,' it said, stretching itself.

The children stood around the hole in a ring, looking at the creature they had found. It was worth looking at. Its eyes were on long horns like a snail's eyes, and it could move them in and out like telescopes; it had ears like a bat's ears, and its tubby body was shaped like a spider's and covered with thick soft fur; its legs and arms were furry too, and it had hands and feet like a monkey's.

'What on earth is it?' Jane said. 'Shall we take it home?'

from VICKY ANGEL

by *Jacqueline Wilson*

'Jade! Oh God, where's Vicky? We got the message. Is she badly hurt? What *happened*?'

'She got knocked over by a car. I . . . she stepped out – she just went straight into it,' I gabble. I hear the squeal of brakes and that one high-pitched scream.

The scream won't stop in my head. It's so loud maybe everyone else can hear it too.

'Knocked over?' says Mrs Waters. 'Oh God. Oh God.'

'Now we mustn't panic. She'll be all right, just you wait and see,' says Mr Waters. He looks at the nurse with me. 'Where is she?'

'Just wait here one second, sir,' she says, and she rushes off.

'We're not waiting! She's our *daughter*!' says Mr Waters and he hurries after her.

Vicky's mum is staring at me.

'Did you get knocked down too, Jade?'

I shake my head.

'It was just Vicky. Like I said, she dashed out –'

'Couldn't you have stopped her?'

She doesn't wait for an answer. She runs after Mr Waters. I stand still. I don't know I'm crying until the nurse comes back and presses a wad of paper hankies into my palm.

'There now, don't worry. She didn't mean it. She didn't even realise what she was saying. She's in shock.'

'But *why* didn't I stop her?' I weep.

'There now. Come on, let's try ringing your mum at work. You need someone to be here for you.'

from THE VOYAGE OF THE DAWN TREADER

by *C. S. Lewis*

The children leave the ship and wander around the island. They cannot see anyone but they hear voices. The Chief Voice explains why they are invisible:

CHIEF VOICE: It's like this. This island has been the property of a great magician time out of mind. And we all are – or perhaps in a manner of speaking, I might say, we were – his servants. Well, to cut a long story short, this magician that I was speaking about, he told us to do something we didn't like. And why not? Because we didn't want to. Well, then, this same magician he fell into a great rage; for I ought to tell you he owned the island and he wasn't used to being crossed. He was terribly downright, you know. But let me see, where am I? Oh yes, this magician then, he goes upstairs (for you must know he kept all his magic things up there and we all lived down below), I say he goes upstairs and puts a spell on us. An uglifying spell. If you saw us now, which in my opinion you may thank your stars you can't, you wouldn't believe what we looked like before we were uglified. You wouldn't really. So there we all were so ugly we couldn't bear to look at one another. So then what did we do? Well, I'll tell you what we did. We waited till we thought this same magician would be asleep in the afternoon and we creep upstairs and go to his magic book, as bold as brass, to see if we can do anything about this uglification. But we were all of a sweat and a tremble, so I won't deceive you. But, believe me or believe me not, I do assure you that we couldn't find anything in the way of a spell for taking off the ugliness. And what with time getting on and being afraid that the old gentleman might wake up any minute – I was all of a muck sweat, so I won't deceive you – well, to cut a long story short, whether we did right or whether we did wrong, in the end we see a spell for making people invisible. And we thought we'd rather be invisible than go on being as ugly as all that. And why? Because we'd like it better.

OR

The children suddenly see a bright light in which a beautiful girl appears. The girl tells them about the three dirty and lifeless figures who are sitting nearby:

GIRL: They came here in a ship whose sails were rags and her timbers ready to fall apart. There were a few others with them, sailors, and when they came to this table one said, 'Here is the good place. Let us set sail and reef sail and row no longer but sit down and end our days in peace!' And the second said, 'No, let us re-embark and sail for Narnia and the west; it may be that Miraz is dead.' But the third, who was a very masterful man, leaped up and said, 'No, by heaven. We are men and Telmarines, not brutes. What should we do but seek adventure after adventure? We have not long to live in any event. Let us spend what is left in seeking the unpeopled world behind the sunrise.' And as they quarrelled he caught up the Knife of Stone which lies there on the table and would have fought with his comrades. But it is a thing not right for him to touch. And as his fingers closed upon the hilt, deep sleep fell upon all the three. And till the enchantment is undone they will never wake.

GRADE 4

SILVER

by *Walter de la Mare*

Slowly, silently, now the moon
Walks the night in her silver shoon;
This way, and that, she peers, and sees
Silver fruit upon silver trees;
One by one the casements catch
Her beams beneath the silvery thatch;
Couched in his kennels, like a log,
With paws of silver sleeps the dog;
From their shadowy cote the white breasts peep
Of doves in a silver-feathered sleep;
A harvest mouse goes scampering by,
With silver claws and silver eye;
And moveless fish in the water gleam,
By silver reeds in a silver stream.

READING ROUND THE CLASS

by *Gervase Phinn*

On Friday we have reading round the class.
Kimberley Bloomer is the best.
She sails slowly along the pages like a great galleon
And everyone looks up and listens.
'Beautiful reading, Kimberley, dear,' sighs Mrs Scott,
'And with such fluency, such feeling.
It's a delight to hear.'

On Friday we have reading round the class.
I'm the worst.
I stumble and mumble along slowly like a broken-down train
And everyone looks up and listens.
Then they smile and snigger and whisper behind their hands.
'Dear me,' sighs Mrs Scott, 'rather rusty, Simon.
Quite a bit of practice needed, don't you think?
Too much television and football, that's your trouble,
And not enough reading.'

And she wonders why I don't like books.

BLUE MONDAY

by *John Kitching*

Mondays I feel I'm useless,
That I'm no use at all –
A damp November firework;
A sad, split tennis ball;
A broken-handled cricket bat;
A rain-bedraggled tabby cat;
A liquid bowl of raspberry jelly,
A single, ancient, smelly welly.
Mondays I just feel useless.

Mondays I feel I'm hopeless –
A pip between the teeth;
A wrinkle in the bedclothes;
The wrestler underneath;
Some summer-soft and runny butter;
A Chinese torture dripping tap;
A blocked and flooded winter gutter;
A trap that's trapped inside a trap.
Mondays I feel just hopeless.

THE FIDDLER OF DOONEY
by *W. B. Yeats*

When I play on my fiddle in Dooney
Folk dance like a wave of the sea;
My cousin is priest in Kilvarnet,
My brother in Moharabuiee.

I pass'd my brother and cousin:
They read in their books of prayer;
I read in my book of songs
I bought at the Sligo fair.

When we come at the end of time.
To Peter sitting in state,
He will smile on the three old spirits,
But call me first through the gate;

For the good are always the merry,
Save by an evil chance;
And the merry love to fiddle,
And the merry love to dance:

And when the folk there spy me,
They will all come up to me,
With 'Here is the fiddler of Dooney!'
And dance like a wave of the sea.

GHOST IN THE SCHOOL
by *Roger Stevens*

Winter dark comes early
And the wind attacks the school building
With a vengeance
Hurling sticks and debris at the walls
Invisible fingers try to widen cracks
To find ways in

In the black windows
I see blazing neon reflections
My pale face
And nothing beyond

I hear the howling wind
I hear the creepy cackle of radiators
And was that the tap of a heel?
The snap of a metre stick?
The click of a latch?
The creak of an opening door?
The snicker-snack of brittle bones?

Quickly now.
I hurry to the main door
Am I all alone
In the building?
Alone with the school ghost?

Why are there no teachers working late tonight?
No stragglers from soccer practice?
Where is the caretaker?
Where are the cleaners?
What was that?
I spin round . . .

THE STOPPER
by *Stanley Cook*

Not in the regular team
But good for a kick-around
On a waste bit of ground
At the end of the street;
Never out of position
In opposition,
Hard and tall
And able to stop
The hottest shot
Without effort
And return the ball
With equal force;
Not great on attack
But the perfect back
That nothing gets past,
Whether slow or fast,
Angled, sliced,
Sidefooted,
Volleyed,
Bounced,
Or overhead;
Strong rather than clever
And apparently fit
To go on for ever –
That red brick wall
Against which you kick
Your ball.

THE TREES
by *Philip Larkin*

The trees are coming into leaf
Like something almost being said;
The recent buds relax and spread,
Their greenness is a kind of grief.

Is it that they are born again
And we grow old? No, they die too.
Their yearly trick of looking new
Is written down in rings of grain.

Yet still the unresting castles thresh
In fullgrown thickness every May.
Last year is dead, they seem to say,
Begin afresh, afresh, afresh.

EARLY WINTER DIARY POEM NOVEMBER 18th 1999
by *Pie Corbett*

Six-thirty;
     winter dawn –

scraping a thin skin
     of frost
from the windscreen –
     numb fingers fumble –
even the spray
     freezes.
The breeze is
     bitter –
It's so cold
     that stones crack –
that wool freezes
     on the sheep's back.

The birds are too still –
     even the sun
turns its back
     on the day;
but lazy wood-smoke
     idles
over Minchin's roof.

40

from MEMORIES OF CHRISTMAS
by *Dylan Thomas*

We reached the black bulk of the house.

'What shall we give them?' Dan whispered.

'*Hark the Herald*? *Christmas comes but Once a Year*?'

'No,' Jack said: 'We'll sing *Good King Wenceslas*. I'll count three.'

One, two, three, and we began to sing, our voices high and seemingly distant in the snow-felted darkness round the house that was occupied by nobody we knew. We stood close together, near the dark door.

> Good King Wenceslas looked out
> On the Feast of Stephen.

And then a small, dry voice, like the voice of someone who has not spoken for a long time, suddenly joined our singing: a small, dry voice from the other side of the door: a small, dry voice through the keyhole. And when we stopped running we were outside *our* house; the front room was lovely and bright; the gramophone was playing; we saw the red and white balloons hanging from the gas-bracket; uncles and aunts sat by the fire; I thought I smelt our supper being fried in the kitchen. Everything was good again, and Christmas shone through all the familiar town.

'Perhaps it was a ghost,' Jim said.

'Perhaps it was trolls,' Dan said, who was always reading.

'Let's go in and see if there's any jelly left,' Jack said. And we did that.

from THE SELFISH GIANT

by *Oscar Wilde*

'I cannot understand why the Spring is so late in coming,' said the Selfish Giant, as he sat at the window and looked out at his cold, white garden; 'I hope there will be a change in the weather.'

But the Spring never came, nor the Summer. The Autumn gave golden fruit to every garden, but to the Giant's garden she gave none. 'He is too selfish,' she said.

One morning the Giant was lying awake in bed when he heard some lovely music. It was really only a little linnet singing outside his window, but it was so long since he had heard a bird sing in his garden that it seemed to him to be the most beautiful music in the world. 'I believe the Spring has come at last,' said the Giant; and he jumped out of bed and looked out.

What did he see?

He saw a most wonderful sight. Through a little hole in the wall the children had crept in, and they were sitting in the branches of the trees. In every tree that he could see there was a little child. And the trees were so glad to have the children back again that they had covered themselves with blossoms. The birds were flying about and twittering with delight, and the flowers were looking up through the green grass and laughing. It was a lovely scene, only in one corner it was still winter. It was the farthest corner of the garden, and in it was standing a little boy. He was so small that he could not reach up to the branches of the tree, and he was wandering all round it, crying bitterly. 'Climb up! little boy,' said the Tree, and it bent its branches down as low as it could; but the boy was too tiny.

And the Giant's heart melted as he looked out. 'How selfish I have been!' he said: 'now I know why the Spring would not come here.'

from THE BAD BEGINNING

by *Lemony Snicket*

'Hello hello hello,' Count Olaf said in a wheezy whisper. He was very tall and very thin, dressed in a grey suit that had many dark stains on it. His face was unshaven, and rather than two eyebrows, like most human beings have, he had just one long one. His eyes were very very shiny, which made him look both hungry and angry. 'Hello, my children. Please step into your new home, and wipe your feet outside so no mud gets indoors.'

As they stepped into the house, Mr Poe behind them, the Baudelaire orphans realised what a ridiculous thing Count Olaf had just said. The room in which they found themselves was the dirtiest they had ever seen, and a little bit of mud from outdoors wouldn't have made a bit of difference. Even by the dim light of the one bare lightbulb that hung from the ceiling, the three children could see that every thing in this room was filthy, from the stuffed head of a lion which was nailed to the wall to the bowl of apple cores which sat on a small wooden table. Klaus willed himself not to cry as he looked around.

'This room looks like it needs a little work,' Mr Poe said, peering around in the gloom.

'I realise that my humble home isn't as fancy as the Baudelaire mansion,' Count Olaf said, 'but perhaps with a bit of your money we could fix it up a little nicer.'

Mr Poe's eyes widened in surprise, and his coughs echoed in the dark room before he spoke. 'The Baudelaire fortune,' he said sternly, 'will not be used for such matters. In fact it will not be used at all, until Violet is of age.'

Count Olaf turned to Mr Poe with a glint in his eye like an angry dog.

from FIVE GO TO SMUGGLER'S TOP

by *Enid Blyton*

George was frightened. She ran to the door, but Mr Lenoir caught her before she opened it. He shook her hard.

'What were you doing in my study? Was it you who knocked and ran away? Do you think it is funny to play tricks like that? I'll soon teach you that it isn't!'

He opened the door and called loudly. 'Block! Come here! Sarah, tell Block I want him.'

Block appeared from the kitchen, his face as blank as usual. Mr Lenoir wrote something down quickly on a piece of paper and gave it to him to read. Block nodded.

'I've told him to take you to your room, lock you in, and give you nothing but bread and water for the rest of the day,' said Mr Lenoir fiercely. 'That will teach you to behave yourself in the future. Any more nonsense and I'll whip you myself.'

'My father won't be very pleased when he hears you're punishing me like this,' began George in a trembling voice. But Mr Lenoir sneered.

'Pah! Wait till he hears from me how you have misbehaved yourself, and I am sure he will agree with me. Now go, and you will not be allowed out of your room till tomorrow. I will make your excuses to your father, when he comes.'

Poor George was propelled upstairs by Block, who was only too delighted to be punishing one of the children. As she came to the door of the room George shouted to the others who were in Julian's room next door.

'Julian! Dick! Help me! Quick, help me!'

from WHISTLE DOWN THE WIND

by *Mary Hayley Bell*

Swallow is in the barn telling the younger children about her meeting with the stranger:

SWALLOW: Can you keep a secret? A really big secret? You've got to hold up your hand and do the 'See this wet' routine:

> See this wet, see this dry,
> Cut my throat if I tell a lie. . . .

This is a great and fabulous secret known to none but those within these walls. You have to join a society to be allowed to know the secret, and all who know must swear never to divulge. Will you absolutely swear? If you ever breathe a word something ghastly will happen to you. . . . Alright. . . . That's Jesus. . . . We have proof. We were in here messing about. There was a sort of knock at the door and I opened it. He stood there smiling at us, and said, 'Knock on the door and it shall be opened unto you.'. . . And I said, 'Who are you?' and he stood staring round this place, not answering at once, and then suddenly said, rather loud: 'JESUS' . . . just like that. . . . His legs were all cut, and his boots and socks crammed with mud and he kind of lurched. I asked Him if I should get someone and He said 'Don't tell them till I've recovered'. . . . He's ill . . . too ill to talk. He's been asleep for six hours! . . . In the daytime! . . . The grown-ups may not believe . . . suppose they try and take Him away . . . after all they did last time. . . . But we can have a gigantic meeting, we can tell them all . . . swear them all to secrecy. There's hundreds of children around here and every child knows other children. We can bring them around here a few at a time to see Him and hear His words. Little by little we can spread the news to children all over the country that the first people to know Jesus has come back will be the children. And . . . if the grown-ups try to take Him away again, we'll defend Him. . . . Hundreds of us!

from MAN IN MOTION

by *Jan Mark*

Lloyd is 14 years old and a great American football enthusiast. He confides in the family's lodger his confusion at some of the outspoken comments of his new friends:

LLOYD: Yes. I have got something on my mind. . . . There's this boy I know, Keith Mainwaring; I met him down at American football, and we got friendly. I mean, we were friends right off, and his dad gives me a lift home afterwards. He's really friendly . . . but he says things, they both do. . . . Racist things. All the time, like without thinking. Every time they see somebody Asian, they say something . . . and I don't say anything. I don't know what to say. I keep thinking they don't really mean it, especially Keith, because he's nice, really, I mean, otherwise he's nice. He rings up and asks how I am, and paid for my lunch and that. I really like him, except for what he says. . . . That's why I've stopped going to practices; to avoid him. I don't think he really means it, I think it's just because of what his dad says. Like my friend Vlad – from school, like he said; if you're sexist it's because you've been brought up to think like that, you never get the chance to work it out. And I don't think Keith knows any Asians. He lives up at the Highbridge end. . . . It's funny . . . ODD . . . calling somebody a racist. It doesn't sound real. We have this lesson at school, Social Awareness Studies, only we call it Isms. Because that's what it is, all the time; sexism, racism, feminism. And last week we had this discussion on racism, somebody brought in a cutting from the newspaper, and everyone said how awful it was. I think most of us are against it . . . Racism was just something on the news . . . . But it's not for me. Not any more.

FOR OLD TIMES' SAKE: A TREE SPEAKS

by *James Kirkup*

I live out my life
in these widening rings
like a thrown stone's ripples
from the centre of things.

I grew with each year
in sunshine and dark;
each ripple expanded
my long coat of bark.

How small my beginnings,
the seed of my heart –
but growing and flowing
with life from the start.

So many bird songs
are caught in my grooves,
and voices, and laughter,
and wild horses' hooves!

I once hid a king
and a highwayman bold;
I've seen thousands of seasons
but don't feel that old.

In winter I'm leafless,
my heart's in my roots.
But when spring comes, the sun
drives new life through my shoots.

I've been struck by the lightning,
been battered by gales;
but through rain, snow and tempest
my faith never fails.

It may be this ring
is the last I shall make,
but I keep the rings turning –
for old times' sake.

PARACHUTE

by *Stanley Snaith*

He poises a moment and looks at the earth far under,
Featureless, small, and those steep miles between;
His spirit shrinks, but he grips and with closed eyes throws
Bodily outward, his breath is snatcht up as he goes
Hurtling, a blunt weight, downward through a tense storm
Of air that numbs him with a dim drug of thunder
Till his being burns dazed as a windy spark.

A pull

That lifts him to an abrupt stillness, and then
Thought clears, his body loosens, glides smooth as a gull
Through deepening calms with smells of the land warm:
The land that grows bright with returning green and gold,
Down to firm, century-anchored earth, to pace
In safety amid the treacheries of space.

MOBILE PHONE
by *Brian Moses*

Hi! It's me, I'm on my mobile phone,
I thought I'd give you a call to say I'm coming back home.

And I know I've got nothing important to say,
but this is my new toy and I love to play . . .

On my mobile phone,
my mobile phone,
wherever I go
I take my mobile phone.

Because without my phone I'm not really here,
I need a mobile phone strapped to my ear.

On the peace and quiet of a country walk,
in a crowded train I just love to talk . . .

On my mobile phone,
my mobile phone,
wherever I go
I take my mobile phone.

And I love to watch people watching me
and thinking how important I must be,

making so many calls and talking so much
with everybody wanting me to keep in touch

On my mobile phone,
my mobile phone,
wherever I go
I take my mobile phone.

And I'm treated well by the phone company
they love sending all their bills to me,

Big, big bills that cost me a lot
but I don't care, I'm a real big shot . . .

On my mobile phone,
my mobile phone,
wherever I go
I take my mobile phone.

STORM IN THE BLACK FOREST
by *D. H. Lawrence*

Now it is almost night, from the bronzey soft sky
jugfull after jugfull of pure white liquid fire, bright white
tipples over and spills down,
and is gone
and gold-bronze flutters beat through the thick upper air.

And as the electric liquid pours out, sometimes
a still brighter white snake wriggles among it spilled
and tumbling wriggling down the sky:
and then the heavens cackle with uncouth sounds.

And the rain won't come, the rain refuses to come!

This is the electricity that man is supposed to have mastered
chained, subjugated to his own use!

supposed to!

LINES WRITTEN ON A SEAT ON THE GRAND CANAL, DUBLIN
by *Patrick Kavanagh*

O commemorate me where there is water,
Canal water preferably, so stilly
Greeny at the heart of summer. Brother
Commemorate me thus beautifully.
Where by a lock niagarously roars
The falls for those who sit in the tremendous silence
Of mid-July. No one will speak in prose
Who finds his way to these Parnassian islands.
A swan goes by head low with many apologies,
Fantastic light looks through the eyes of bridges –
And look! a barge comes bringing from Athy
And other far-flung towns mythologies.
O commemorate me with no hero-courageous
Tomb – just a canal-bank seat for the passer-by.

AFTER WE'VE GONE
by *Fran Landesman*

Who will live in our house
After we've gone
Will they have green plastic
Instead of a lawn?

Who will live in our house
After the wars?
Will there be mutations
That crawl on all fours?

Will the shiny robot workers
Be dreaming strange, new dreams?
Will the pigeons, big as turkeys
Roost on our ancient beams?

Who will use our kitchen?
What will they cook?
Who will sleep in our room
And how will they look?

Will they feel our ghosts disturbing
Their cybernetic years
With the echoes of our laughter
And the shadows of our tears?

Will there still be lovers?
Who will sing our songs?
Who will live in our house
After we've gone?

THATCHER
by *Seamus Heaney*

Bespoke for weeks, he turned up some morning
Unexpectedly, his bicycle slung
With a light ladder and a bag of knives.
He eyed the old rigging, poked at the eaves,

Opened and handled sheaves of lashed wheat-straw.
Next, the bundled rods: hazel and willow
Were flicked for weight, twisted in case they'd snap.
It seemed he spent the morning warming up:

Then fixed the ladder, laid out well honed blades
And snipped at straw and sharpened ends of rods
That, bent in two, made a white-pronged staple
For pinning down his world, handful by handful.

Couchant for days on sods above the rafters
He shaved and flushed the butts, stitched all together
Into a sloped honeycomb, a stubble patch,
And left them gaping at his Midas touch.

THE BLOB
by *Wes Magee*

And . . . and what is it like?
      Oh, it's scary and fatbumped
      and spike-eared and groany.
      It's hairy and face-splumped
      and bolshie and bony.

And . . . and where does it live?
      Oh, in comets and spaceships
      and pulsars and blackholes.
      In craters and sheepdips
      and caverns and northpoles.

And . . . and what does it eat?
      Oh, roast rocks and fishlegs
      and x-rays and mooncrust.
      hen steelmeat and sun-eggs
      and lava and spacedust.

And . . . and who are its enemies?
      Oh, Zonkers and Moonquakes
      and Sunquarks and Zigbags.
      Dumb Duncers and Milkshakes
      and Smogsters and Wigwags.

And . . . and what does it wear?
      Not a thing! It's bare!

from HAPHAZARD HOUSE

by *Mary Wesley*

Stillness. We gathered close together in the road. I had never experienced stillness. The quiet was awesome. My tired ears, full of the sound of traffic and the Mini's engine, took a while to adjust.

Then I heard the cooling engines click, and Victoria sigh. There was a full moon. The shadow of a church tower fell across our group. The church clock ticked, the minute hand jerked, the clock whirred, then struck twice.

The square was small; four roads led from it. On tiptoe Josh and I explored. There was a post office and general store, and that was all in the way of shops. The village was very small, the church of cathedral proportions. We went back to the others.

'Which way now?' Even Grandpa didn't speak above a whisper.

'I don't know.' Pa tipped the hat to the back of his head.

'We cannot wake anybody at this hour,' whispered Ma.

'Why not?' Grandpa looked worn out.

'Darling, just look at us.' Ma grinned. I could see her teeth in the moonlight. 'We'd make an awful impression. We look like a pop festival in this van. Or refugees.'

'Maybe, but we must ask where Haphazard is. We can't spend the rest of the night here.'

from A CHIP IN THE SUGAR

by *Alan Bennett*

Now the café we generally patronise is just that bit different. It's plain but it's classy, no cloths on the tables, the menu comes on a little slate and the waitresses wear their own clothes and look as if they're doing it just for the fun of it. The stuff's all home-made and we're both big fans of the date and walnut bread. I said, 'This is the place.' Mr Turnbull goes straight past. 'No,' he says, 'I know somewhere, just opened. Press on.'

Now if there's one thing Mother and me are agreed on it's that red is a common colour. And the whole place is done out in red. Lampshades red. Waitresses in red. Plates red, and on the tables those plastic sauce things got up to look like tomatoes. Also red. And when I look there's a chip in the sugar. I thought, 'Mother won't like this.' 'Oh,' she says, 'this looks cheerful, doesn't it, Graham?' I said, 'There's a chip in the sugar.' 'A detail,' he says, 'they're still having their teething troubles. Is it three coffees?' I said, 'We like tea,' only Mother says, 'No. I feel like an adventure. I'll have coffee.' He gets hold of the menu and puts his hand on hers. 'Might I suggest,' he says, 'a cheeseburger?' She said, 'Oh, what's that?' He said, 'It's fresh country beef, mingled with golden-fried onions, topped off with toasted cheese served with french fries and lemon wedge.' 'Oh, lemon wedge,' said Mother. 'That sounds nice.' I thought, 'Well, I hope you can keep it down. Because it'll be the pizza story all over again. One mouthful and at four o' clock in the morning I was still stuck at her bedside with the bucket. She said, 'I like new experiences in eating. I had a pizza once, didn't I, Graham?' I didn't say anything.

from THE EUSTACE DIAMONDS

by *Anthony Trollope*

'What is this about the diamonds?' he asked as soon as he saw her. She had flown almost into his arms, as though carried there by the excitement of the moment. 'You don't really mean that they have been stolen?'

'I do, Frank.'

'On the journey?'

'Yes, Frank; – at the inn at Carlisle.'

'Box and all?' Then she told him the whole story; – not the true story, but the story as it was believed by all the world. She found it to be impossible to tell him the true story. 'And the box was broken open, and left in the street?'

'Under an archway,' said Lizzie.

'And what do the police think?'

'I don't know what they think. Lord George says that they believe he is the thief.'

'He knew of them,' said Frank, as though he imagined that the suggestion was not altogether absurd.

'Oh, yes; – he knew of them.'

'And what is to be done?'

'I don't know. I've sent for you to tell me.' Then Frank averred that information should be immediately given to Mr Camperdown. He would himself call Mr Camperdown, and would also see the head of the police. He did not doubt that all the circumstances were already known in London at the police office; – but it might be well that he should see the officer. He was acquainted with the gentleman, and might perhaps learn something. Lizzie at once acceded, and Frank went direct to Mr Camperdown's offices. 'If I had lost ten thousand pounds in that way,' said Mrs Carbuncle, 'I think I should have broken my heart.' Lizzie felt that her heart was bursting rather than being broken, because the ten thousand pounds' worth of diamonds was not really lost.

from THE LAST BATTLE

by *C. S. Lewis*

Lucy looked hard at the garden and saw that it was not really a garden but a whole world, with its own rivers and woods and sea and mountains. But they were not strange: she knew them all.

'I see,' she said. 'This is still Narnia, and more real and more beautiful than the Narnia down below, just as *it* was more real and more beautiful than the Narnia outside the stable door! I see. . . world within world, Narnia within Narnia. . .'

'Yes,' said Mr Tumnus, 'like an onion: except that as you go in and in, each circle is larger than the last.'

And Lucy looked this way and that and soon found that a new and beautiful thing had happened to her. Whatever she looked at, however far away it might be, once she had fixed her eyes steadily on it, became quite clear and close as if she were looking through a telescope. She could see the whole Southern desert and beyond it the great city of Tashbaan: to Eastward she could see Cair Paravel on the edge of the sea and the very window of the room that had been her own. And far out to sea she could discover the islands, islands after islands to the end of the world, and, beyond the end, the huge mountain which they had called Aslan's country. But now she saw that it was part of a great chain of mountains which ringed round the whole world. In front of her it seemed to come quite close. Then she looked to her left and saw what she took to be a great bank of brightly-coloured cloud, cut off from them by a gap. But she looked harder and saw that it was not a cloud at all but a real land. And when she had fixed her eyes on one particular spot of it, she at once cried out, 'Peter! Edmund! Come and look! Come quickly.' And they came and looked, for their eyes also had become like hers.

'Why!' exclaimed Peter. 'It's England. And that's the house itself — Professor Kirk's old home in the country where all our adventures began!'

from NOAH

by *Andre Obey*

Noah sits thinking as the rain pours down and the beasts howl below. He talks to himself:

NOAH: I thought to-day would never end. It's seemed so long. One felt it wouldn't go unless one gave it a push. Ouch! Well, it's over now. Let me see. . . . That makes exactly forty days! I wonder how many there'll be altogether. Fifty, sixty, eighty? People are funny, always thinking everything will turn out just as they expect – why, I scolded them just now for trying to look ahead, and here I am doing it myself. Well, I suppose I was right to scold them, but it's not so easy when it comes to yourself. Hullo! Now who's snoring? Oh, mother, bless her heart, and she still says she's never snored in her life. Oh, well, she's tired out, poor thing. They all are, tired and anxious, that's why they squabble and complain. They're good children really, though. Yes, there's nothing wrong with this cargo . . . not even Ham. He wants to seem grown-up, that's why he plays the fool. Oh, it's a fine cargo! When we get to harbour, and they're all lined up on the quay – I can see it now – a big white quay all shining in the sunlight – and God says to me 'claim your reward, Noah,' then I'll say to Him, 'Lord, all I want is to parade my flock. Look at them: how fine and strong the people are. And how well the beasts are looking. There isn't a penny-worth of disease or wickedness in the whole world. The men are all laughing, and the animals would be laughing too, if they knew how.' And He'll begin to laugh Himself, and He'll laugh so loud He'll knock us all sprawling. Ha, ha.

from A BOSTON STORY

by *Ronald Gow (from the novel by Henry James)*

Tomboyish Nora is 16 years old and the adopted daughter of Roger. They talk by the fire:

NORA: (*at the window*) Yes. It is still snowing. It's all white outside. And very silent. It makes me feel that you and I are alone in the world . . . (*Reacting to a remark he makes.*) . . . I'm not YOUR little girl. . . . No, Roger, I'm not. I'm no one's little girl. Do you think I can't remember. . . . (*Sits on the floor beside him.*) Sometimes I'm frightened. . . . Roger – suppose I only exist in your mind. That I'm not a person at all. That I'm nobody. . . .

NO! I don't belong to you! I want to be my own father's daughter. And my mother's too. I haven't spoken of them before. You must please let me tonight. You must talk to me about my father. Was he wicked? You never mentioned his name. He can do no harm, now he's dead, can he? We oughtn't to despise him – forget him altogether? Ought we? . . . I can remember that he took his own life . . . in that hotel in New York. . . . (*She looks into fire.*) There were some palms and a big staircase. . . . If I ever go back to New York I shall go and look for it. . . . Because it's the only home I can remember. . . Tell me – wasn't he wonderfully handsome? . . . (*Roger agrees.*) He used to play the piano and there was a great deal of singing. My mother used to sing, I'm sure. I can't remember her. . . . Poor dead things! Well, so much for the past. . . . Do you know, girls at school were always talking about their homes, and their fathers and their mothers. They seemed so much more real than I did. . . . I shall learn everything you order me to learn. I shall be everything you want me to be. (*Kisses him gravely, then turns away.*) Oh, how I wish I were pretty! . . . If you're satisfied, I suppose I am. It looks hopeless to me.

THE VOICE

by *Thomas Hardy (1840-1928)*

Woman much missed, how you call to me, call to me,
Saying that now you are not as you were
When you had changed from the one who was all to me,
But as at first, when our day was fair.

Can it be you that I hear? Let me view you, then,
Standing as when I drew near to the town
Where you would wait for me: yes, as I knew you then,
Even to the original air-blue gown!

Or is it only the breeze, in its listlessness
Travelling across the wet mead to me here,
You being ever dissolved to wan wistlessness,
Heard no more again far or near?

   Thus I; faltering forward,
   Leaves around me falling,
Wind oozing thin through the thorn from norward
   And the woman calling.

JOINING THE COLOURS
(WEST KENTS, DUBLIN 1914)

by *Katharine Tynan (1861-1931)*

There they go marching all in step so gay!
   Smooth-cheeked and golden, food for shells and guns.
Blithely they go as to a wedding day,
     The mothers' sons.

The drab street stares to see them row on row
   On the high tram-tops, singing like the lark.
Too careless-gay for courage, singing they go
     Into the dark.

With tin whistles, mouth-organs, any noise,
   They pipe the way to glory and the grave;
Foolish and young, the gay and golden boys
     Love cannot save.

High heart! High courage! The poor girls they kissed
   Run with them: they shall kiss no more, alas!
Out of the mist they stepped – into the mist
     Singing they pass.

ENGINEERS' CORNER
by *Wendy Cope (1945-)*

*Why isn't there an Engineers' Corner in Westminster
Abbey? In Britain we've always made more fuss of
a ballad than a blueprint. . .*

*How many schoolchildren dream of becoming great
engineers?*

Advertisement placed in The Times
by the Engineering Council

We make more fuss of ballads than of blueprints –
That's why so many poets end up rich,
While engineers scrape by in cheerless garrets.
Who needs a bridge or dam? Who needs a ditch?

Whereas the person who can write a sonnet
Has got it made. It's always been the way,
For everybody knows that we need poems
And everybody reads them every day.

Yes, life is hard if you choose engineering –
You're sure to need another job as well;
You'll have to plan your projects in the evenings
Instead of going out. It must be hell.

While well-heeled poets ride around in Daimlers,
You'll burn the midnight oil to earn a crust,
With no hope of a statue in the Abbey,
With no hope, even, of a modest bust.

No wonder small boys dream of writing couplets
And spurn the bike, the lorry and the train.
There's far too much encouragement for poets –
That's why this country's going down the drain.

TO MISTRESS ANNE
by *John Skelton (1460-1529)*

Mistress Anne,
I am your man,
As you may well espy.
If you will be
Content with me,
I am your man.

But if you will
Keep company still
With every knave that comes by,
Then you will be
Forsaken of me,
That am your man.

But if you fain,
I tell you plain,
If I presently shall die,
I will not such
As loves too much,
That am your man.

For if you can
Love every man
That can flatter and lie,
Then are ye
No match for me,
That am your man.

For I will not take
No such kind of make
(May all full well it try!),
But off will ye cast
At any blast,
That am your man.

ANIMAL TRANQUILITY AND DECAY
by *William Wordsworth (1770-1850)*

The little hedgerow birds,
That peck along the road, regard him not.
He travels on, and in his face, his step,
His gait, is one expression: every limb,
His look and bending figure, all bespeak
A man who does not move with pain, but moves
With thought. – He is insensibly subdued
To settled quiet: he is one by whom
All effort seems forgotten; one to whom
Long patience hath such mild composure given,
That patience now doth seem a thing of which
He hath no need. He is by nature led
To peace so perfect that the young behold
With envy, what the Old Man hardly feels.

THE HEAVENLY CITY
by *Stevie Smith (1902-1971)*

I sigh for the heavenly country,
Where the heavenly people pass,
And the sea is as quiet as a mirror
Of beautiful, beautiful glass.

I walk in the heavenly field,
With lilies and poppies bright,
I am dressed in a heavenly coat
Of polished white.

When I walk in the heavenly parkland
My feet on the pastures are bare,
Tall waves the grass, but no harmful
Creature is there.

At night I fly over the housetops,
And stand on the bright moony beams;
Gold are all heaven's rivers,
And silver her streams.

WHY SO PALE AND WAN?

by *Sir John Suckling (1609-1642)*

Why so pale and wan, fond lover?
    Prithee, why so pale?
Will, when looking well can't move her,
    Looking ill prevail?
    Prithee, why so pale?

Why so dull and mute, young sinner?
    Prithee, why so mute?
Will, when speaking well can't win her,
    Saying nothing do 't?
    Prithee, why so mute?

Quit, quit for shame! This will not move;
    This cannot take her.
If of herself she will not love,
    Nothing can make her:
    The devil take her!

from ELEGY WRITTEN IN A COUNTRY CHURCHYARD

by *Thomas Gray (1716-1771)*

The curfew tolls the knell of parting day,
    The lowing herd wind slowly o'er the lea,
The plowman homeward plods his weary way,
    And leaves the world to darkness and to me.

Now fades the glimmering landscape on the sight,
    And all the air a solemn stillness holds,
Save where the beetle wheels his droning flight,
    And drowsy tinklings lull the distant folds;

Save that from yonder ivy-mantled tower
    The moping owl does to the moon complain
Of such as, wand'ring near her secret bower,
    Molest her ancient solitary reign.

Beneath those rugged elms, that yew-tree's shade,
    Where heaves the turf in many a mould'ring heap,
Each in his narrow cell for ever laid,
    The rude forefathers of the hamlet sleep.

from CLAUDIUS THE GOD

by *Robert Graves (1895-1985)*

'They could be and ought to be useful. But they do great harm by their lack of co-operation and their insane jealous competition. The word goes round, for example, that there's to be a demand for coloured marble from Phrygia, or Syrian silk, or ivory from Africa, or Indian pepper; and for fear of missing a chance they scramble for the market like mad dogs. Instead of persisting with their ordinary lines of commerce, they rush their ships to the new centre of excitement, with orders to their captains to bring as much marble, pepper, silk, or ivory as possible at whatever cost, and then of course the foreigners raise the prices. Two hundred shiploads of pepper or silk are brought home at great expense when there is really only demand for twenty, and the hundred and eighty ships could have been far better employed in importing other things for which there would have been a demand and for which a fair price could have been got. Obviously trade ought to be centrally controlled in the same way as armies and law-courts and religion and everything else is controlled.'

from A HANDFUL OF DUST

by *Evelyn Waugh (1903-1966)*

Marjorie had her hat on and was sitting at her writing-table puzzling over her cheque-book and a sheaf of bills.

'Darling, what *does* the country do to you? You look like a thousand pounds. Where *did* you get that suit?'

'I don't know. Some shop.'

'What's the news at Hetton?'

'All the same. Tony madly feudal. John Andrew cursing like a stable boy.'

'And you?'

'Me? Oh, I'm all right.'

'Who's been to stay?'

'No one. We had a friend of Tony's called Mr Beaver last week-end.'

'John Beaver? . . . How very odd. I shouldn't have thought he was at all Tony's ticket.'

'He wasn't. . . . What's he like?'

'I hardly know him. I see him at Margot's sometimes. He's a great one for going everywhere.'

'I thought he was rather pathetic.'

'Oh, he's *pathetic* all right. D'you fancy him?'

'Heavens, no.'

from ORLANDO

by *Virginia Woolf (1882-1941)*

The Great Frost was, historians tell us, the most severe that has ever visited these islands. Birds froze in mid-air and fell like stones to the ground. . . .

But while the country people suffered the extremity of want, and the trade of the country was at a standstill, London enjoyed a carnival of the utmost brilliancy. The Court was at Greenwich, and the new King seized the opportunity that his coronation gave him to curry favour with the citizens. He directed that the river, which was frozen to a depth of twenty feet and more for six or seven miles on either side, should be swept, decorated and given all the semblance of a park or pleasure ground, with arbours, mazes, alleys, drinking booths, etc., at his expense. . . . Coloured balloons hovered motionless in the air. Here and there burnt vast bonfires of cedar and oak wood, lavishly salted, so that the flames were of green, orange, and purple fire. But however fiercely they burnt, the heat was not enough to melt the ice which, though of singular transparency, was yet of the hardness of steel. So clear indeed was it that there could be seen, congealed at a depth of several feet, here a porpoise, there a flounder. Shoals of eels lay motionless in a trance, but whether their state was one of death or merely of suspended animation which the warmth would revive puzzled the philosophers. Near London Bridge, where the river had frozen to a depth of some twenty fathoms, a wrecked wherry boat was plainly visible, lying on the bed of the river where it had sunk last autumn, overladen with apples. The old bumboat woman, who was carrying her fruit to market on the Surrey side, sat there in her plaids and farthingales with her lap full of apples, for all the world as if she were about to serve a customer, though a certain blueness about the lips hinted the truth. . . . But it was at night that the carnival was at its merriest. For the frost continued unbroken; the nights were of perfect stillness; the moon and stars blazed with the hard fixity of diamonds and to the fine music of flute and trumpet the courtiers danced.

from THE SEVEN CREAM JUGS

by *Saki* [*H. H. Munro*] *(1870-1916)*

Wilfred Pigeoncote had suddenly become heir to his uncle, Sir Wilfrid Pigeoncote, on the death of his cousin, Major Wilfrid Pigeoncote, who had succumbed to the after-effects of a polo accident. (A Wilfrid Pigeoncote had covered himself with honours in the course of Marlborough's campaigns, and the name Wilfrid had been a baptismal weakness in the family ever since.) The new heir to the family dignity and estates was a young man of about five-and-twenty, who was known more by reputation than by person to a wide circle of cousins and kinsfolk. And the reputation was an unpleasant one. The numerous other Wilfrids in the family were distinguished one from another chiefly by the names of their residences or professions, as Wilfrid of Hubbledown, and young Wilfrid the Gunner, but this particular scion was known by the ignominious and expressive label of Wilfrid the Snatcher. From his late schooldays onward he had been possessed by an acute and obstinate form of kleptomania; he had the acquisitive instinct of the collector without any of the collector's discrimination. Anything that was smaller and more portable than a sideboard, and above the value of ninepence, had an irresistable attraction for him, provided that it fulfilled the necessary condition of belonging to some one else. On the rare occasions when he was included in a country-house party, it was usual and almost necessary for his host, or some member of the family, to make a friendly inquisition through his baggage on the eve of his departure, to see if he had packed up 'by mistake' any one else's property. The search usually produced a large and varied yield.

from THE VOYSEY INHERITANCE

by *Harley Granville Barker (1877-1946)*

MAJOR BOOTH VOYSEY: I am beginning to think that you have worked yourself into rather an hysterical state over this unhappy business. The simple question before us is . . . what is the best course to pursue? . . . In so far as our poor father was dishonest to his clients, I pray that he may be forgiven. In so far as he spent his life honestly endeavouring to right a wrong which he had found already committed . . . I forgive him . . . I admire him, Edward . . . and I feel it my duty to – er – reprobate most strongly the – er – gusto with which you have been holding him up in memory to us . . . ten minutes after we'd been standing round his grave . . . as a monster of wickedness. I think I knew him as well as you . . . better. And . . . thank God! . . . there was not between him and me this . . . this unhappy business to warp my judgment of him. Did you ever know a more charitable man . . . a larger-hearted? He was a faithful husband . . . and what a father to all of us! . . . putting us out into the world and fully intending to leave us comfortably settled there. Further . . . as I see this matter, Edward . . . when as a young man he was told this terrible secret and entrusted with such a frightful task . . . did he turn his back on it like a coward? No. He went through it heroically to the end of his life. And, as he died, I imagine there was no more torturing thought than that he had left his work unfinished. And now . . . if all these clients can be kept receiving their natural incomes . . . and if father's plan could be carried out, of gradually replacing the capital . . .

from THE DAUGHTER-IN-LAW

by *D. H. Lawrence (1885-1930)*

MRS PURDY: But it's no use throwin' good words after bad deeds. Not but what it's a nasty thing for yer t'r 'a done, it is – an' yer can scarce look your missis i' th' face again, I should think. (*Pause.*) But I says t'r our Bertha, 'It's his'n, an' he mun pay!' Eh, but how 'er did but scraight an' cry. It fair turned me ower. 'Dunna go to 'm, Mother,' 'er says, 'dunna go to 'm for to tell him!' 'Yi,' I says, 'right's right – tha doesna get off wi' nowt, nor shall 'e neither. 'E wor but a scamp to do such a thing,' I says, yes, I did. For you was older nor 'er. Not but what she was old enough ter ha'e more sense. But 'er wor allers one o' th' come-day-go-day sort, as 'ud gi'e th' clothes off 'er back an' niver know 'er wor nek'd – a gr'at soft looney as she is, an' serves 'er right for bein' such a gaby. Yi, an' I believe 'er wor fond on thee – if a wench can be fond of a married man. For one blessing, 'er doesna know what 'er wor an' what 'er worn't. For they mau talk o' bein' i' love – but you non in love wi' onybody, wi'out they's a chance o' their marryin' you – howiver much you may like 'em. An' I'm thinkin', th' childt'll set 'er up again when it comes, for 'er's gone that wezzel-brained an' doited, I'm sure! An' it's a mort o' trouble for me, mester, a sight o' trouble it is. Not as I s'll be hard on 'er. She knowed I wor comin' 'ere to-night, an's not spoke a word for hours. I left 'er sittin' on th' sofey hangin' 'er 'ead. But it's a weary business, mester, an' nowt ter be proud on. I s'd think tha wishes tha'd niver clapt eyes on our Bertha.

from A PHOENIX TOO FREQUENT

by *Christopher Fry (1907-2005)*

DOTO: Nothing but the harmless day gone into black

Is all the dark is. And so what's my trouble?

Demons is so much wind. Are so much wind.

I've plenty to fill my thoughts. All that I ask

Is don't keep turning men over in my mind,

Venerable Aphrodite. I've had my last one

And thank you. I thank thee. He smelt of sour grass

And was likeable. He collected ebony quoits.

(An owl hoots near at hand.)

O Zeus! O some god or other, where is the oil?

Fire's from Prometheus. I thank thee. If I

Mean to die I'd better see what I'm doing.

*(She fills the lamp with oil. The flame burns
up rightly and shows Dynamene, beautiful
and young, leaning asleep beside a bier.)*

Honestly, I would rather have to sleep

With a bald bee-keeper who was wearing his boots

Than spend more days fasting and thirsting and crying

In a tomb. I shouldn't have said that. Pretend

I didn't hear myself. But life and death

Is cat and dog in this double-bed of a world.

My master, my poor master, was a man

Whose nose was as straight as a little buttress,

And now he has taken it to Elysium

Where it won't be noticed among all the other straightness.

(The owl cries again and wakens Dynamene.)

Oh, them owls. Those owls. It's woken her.

from CHIPS WITH EVERYTHING

by *Arnold Wesker (1932-)*

CHAS: What they say, Pip? What they want you for, what did they say? Hell, look at your face, did they beat you? Did they make you use the bayonet? They did, didn't they? I can tell it from your face. You're crying – are you crying? Want a cigarette? Here, have a cigarette. The others have all gone to the Naafi, it's New Year's Eve, gone for a big booze-up. Bloody fools – all they do is drink. I think I'll give it up, me. Well, what did they say, man – talk to me? You know why I didn't go to the Naafi – I – I was waiting for you. It seemed fishy them calling you in the evening, so I waited to see. Pip? I'm telling you I waited for you. I wanted to tell you something. I want to ask you a favour; I've been meaning all these last days to ask you this favour. You see – you know me, don't you, you know the sort of bloke . . . I'm – I'm not dumb, I'm not a fool, I'm not a real fool, not a bloody moron and I thought, well, I thought maybe you could, could teach me – something, anything. Eh? Well, not anything but something proper, real. . . .

I can't read books, but I can listen to you. Maybe we'll get posted to the same place, and then every evening, or every other evening, or once a week, even, you could talk to me a bit, for half an hour say. Remember how you talked that night about your grandfathers, about all those inventions and things. Well, I liked that, I listened to that, I could listen all night to that. Only I want to know about something else, I want to know about – I don't even know how to put it, about – you know, you know the word, about business and raw materials and people working and selling things – you know, there's a word for it – . . .

Enocomics – that's it.

from THE ARISTOCRATS

by *Brian Friel (1929-)*

CASIMIR: Oh, there are. Oh, yes, there are – aren't there? Yes – yes, I discovered a great truth when I was nine. No, not a great truth; but I made a great discovery when I was nine – not even a great discovery but an important, a very important discovery for me. I suddenly realised I was different from other boys. When I say I was different I don't mean – you know – good Lord, I don't for a second mean I was – you know – as they say nowadays 'homo-sexual' – good heavens I must admit, if anything, Eamon, if anything I'm – (*Looks around.*) – I'm vigorously hetero-sexual ha-ha. But of course I don't mean that either. No, no. But anyway. What I discovered was that for some reason people found me . . . peculiar. Of course I sensed it first from the boys at boarding school. But it was Father with his usual – his usual directness and honesty who made me face it. I remember the day he said to me: 'Had you been born down there' – we were in the library and he pointed down to Ballybeg – 'Had you been born down there, you'd have become the village idiot. Fortunately for you, you were born here and we can absorb you.' Ha-ha. So at nine years of age I knew certain things: that certain kinds of people laughed at me; that the easy relationships that other men enjoy would always elude me; that – that – that I would never succeed in life, whatever – you know – whatever 'succeed' means –

65

from PHILADELPHIA, HERE I COME!

by *Brian Friel (1929-)*

MADGE: (*Looking at case*)

Tomorrow'll be sore on him (*Gar*): his heart'll break tomorrow, and all next week, and the week after maybe . . . Brigid – aye, it's all right – (*Trying out the sound of the name*) Brigid – Biddy – Biddy Mulhern – Brigid Mulhern – aye – like Madge Mulhern doesn't sound right – (*Trying it out*) – Madge Mulhern – Madge Mulhern – I don't know – It's too aul'-fashioned or something . . . Has he his cap? (*Finds it in the pocket of the coat. Also finds an apple.*) . . . Aye, he has. And an apple, if you don't mind – for all his grief. He'll be all right. That Lizzy one'll look after him well, I suppose, if she can take time off from blatherin'. Garden front and back, and a TV in the house of lords – I'll believe them things when I see them! Never had much time for blatherin' women . . . (*Remembering*) An envelope . . . (*She takes two notes from her pocket, goes to the dresser, and finds an envelope. She puts the money into the envelope, and slips the envelope into the coat pocket.*) That'll get him a cup of tea on the plane. I had put them two pounds by me to get my feet done on the fair day. But I can wait till next month. From what I hear, there's no big dances between now and then . . . (*She stands looking at the bedroom door.*) So. I think that's everything . . . (*She raises her hand in a sort of vague benediction, then shuffles towards the scullery.*) When the boss was his (*Gar's*) age, he was the very same as him: leppin, and eejitin' about and actin' the clown; as like as two peas. And when he's (*Gar*) the age the boss is now, he'll turn out just the same. And although I won't be here to see it, you'll find that he's learned nothin' in-between times. That's people for you – they'd put you astray in the head if you thought long enough about them.

from ABSURD PERSON SINGULAR

by *Alan Ayckbourn (1939-)*

JANE: Mrs Jackson, are you all right? You shouldn't be on the cold floor in your condition, you know. You should be in bed. Surely? Here. . .

(*She helps Eva to her feet and steers her back to the table.*)

Now, you sit down here. Don't you worry about that oven now. That oven can wait. You clean it later. No point in damaging your health for an oven, is there? Mind you, I know just what you feel like, though. You suddenly get that urge, don't you? You say, I must clean that oven if it kills me. I shan't sleep, I shan't eat till I've cleaned that oven. It haunts you. I know just that feeling. I'll tell you what I'll do. Never say I'm not a good neighbour – shall I have a go at it for you? How would that be? Would you mind? I mean, it's no trouble for me. I quite enjoy it, actually – and you'd do the same for me, wouldn't you? Right. That's settled. No point in wasting time, let's get down to it. Now then, what are we going to need? Bowl of water, got any oven cleaner, have you? Never mind, we'll find it – I hope you're not getting cold, you look very peaky. (*Hunting under the sink.*) Now then, oven cleaner? Have we got any? Well, if we haven't, we'll just have to use our old friend Mr Vim, won't we? (*She rummages.*)

from IN LAMBETH

by *Jack Shepherd (1940-)*

Blake starts to change, whistling to himself. After a few moments he turns to the audience.

BLAKE: Hello. You mustn't think that we make a habit of this sort of thing – throwing off our clothes whenever the sun comes out – and entertaining strangers without a stitch on, and so on . . . The climate's against it for one thing. And for most of the time, I'm afraid, the inclination just isn't there. No . . . on the *surface*, our lives are fairly ordinary. Hum-drum. Our pleasure is very often in our work and my nature is such that for much of the time I keep no company other than my own.

[Mrs Blake: (*off*) William!]

There's a story about that. An apocryphal story. Catherine was talking to someone, *who* I don't know . . . 'And how is Mr Blake?' they enquired. 'I'm not sure,' my wife replied, 'he is so often in paradise these days'. . . . Or something like that. It's probably not even true. You know how these stories get around.

[Mrs Blake: (*off*) William! Hurry Up!]

(*Examines his clothes*) It's *strange* wearing clothes, isn't it? We get so used to it we lose our sense of wonder and start thinking that the clothed state is the *natural* one. Which it isn't. Besides, we look so *vulnerable* without them, like crabs without their shells. It's as if there's something missing from the original design, something that would enable us to endure the summer sun and the winter cold . . . without having to resort to these. (*Touching them.*) Layers of clothes.

[Mrs Blake: (*appearing at the door*) William. It's *you* he wants to talk to.]

I'm *serious*. Well . . . almost. The form of man is *perfect*, isn't it? (*Touching himself.*) Head. Body. Arms. Legs . . . genitals. Perfect. (*Standing as in 'Glad Day'.*) Who could seriously imagine us other than the way we are? God made us, after all, in *his* image.

GRADE 7

LEAVE ME, O LOVE!
by *Sir Philip Sidney (1554-1586)*

Leave me, O Love, which reachest but to dust,
And thou, my mind, aspire to higher things;
Grow rich in that which never taketh rust:
Whatever fades, but fading pleasure brings.
Draw in thy beams, and humble all thy might
To that sweet yoke where lasting freedoms be,
Which breaks the clouds and opens forth the light
That doth both shine and give us sight to see.
Oh, take fast hold! Let that light be thy guide
In this small course which birth draws out to death,
And think how evil becometh him to slide
Who seeketh heaven, and comes of heavenly breath.
     Then, farewell, world! thy uttermost I see.
     Eternal Love, maintain thy life in me!

OH, THE MONTH OF MAY!
by *Thomas Dekker (c.1570-1632)*

Oh, the month of May, the merry month of May,
So frolic, so gay, and so green, so green, so green!
Oh, and then did I unto my true Love say,
Sweet Peg, thou shalt be my Summer's Queen.

Now the nightingale, the pretty nightingale,
The sweetest singer in all the forest's quire,
Entreats thee, sweet Peggy, to hear thy true Love's tale:
Lo, yonder she sitteth, her breast against a brier.

But oh, I spy the cuckoo, the cuckoo, the cuckoo;
See where she sitteth; come away, my joy:
Come away, I prithee, I do not like the cuckoo
Should sing where my Peggy and I kiss and toy.

Oh, the month of May, the merry month of May,
So frolic, so gay, and so green, so green, so green;
And then did I unto my true Love say,
Sweet Peg, thou shalt be my Summer's Queen.

from PARADISE LOST
by *John Milton (1608-1674)*

Of Mans First Disobedience, and the Fruit
Of that Forbidden Tree, whose mortal taste
Brought Death into the World, and all our woe,
With loss of *Eden*, till one greater Man
Restore us, and regain the blissful Seat,
Sing Heav'nly Muse, that on the secret top
Of *Oreb*, or of *Sinai*, didst inspire
That Shepherd, who first taught the chosen Seed,
In the Beginning how the Heav'ns and Earth
Rose out of *Chaos*: or if *Sion* Hill
Delight thee more, and *Siloa's* Brook that flow'd
Fast by the Oracle of God; I thence
Invoke thy aid to my adventrous Song,
That with no middle flight intends to soar
Above th' *Aonian* Mount, while it pursues
Things unattempted yet in Prose or Rhime.
And chiefly Thou O Spirit, that dost préfer
Before all Temples th' upright heart and pure,
Instruct me, for Thou know'st; Thou from the first
Wast present, and with mighty wings outspread
Dove-like satst brooding on the vast Abyss
And mad'st it pregnant: What in me is dark
Illumine, what is low raise and support;
That to the highth of this great Argument
I may assert Eternal Providence,
And justifie the wayes of God to men.

SONG: TO CELIA
by *Ben Jonson (c.1572-1637)*

Kiss me, sweet; the wary lover
Can your favours keep, and cover,
When the common courting jay
All your bounties will betray.
Kiss again; no creature comes.
Kiss, and score up wealthy sums
On my lips thus hardly sund'red
While you breathe. First give a hundred,
Then a thousand, then another
Hundred, then unto the tother
Add a thousand, and so more
Till you equal with the store
All the grass that Rumney yields,
Or the sands in Chelsea fields,
Or the drops in silver Thames,
Or the stars that gild his streams
In the silent summer nights
When youths ply their stol'n delights:
That the curious may not know
How to tell them as they flow;
And the envious, when they find
What their number is, be pined.

WHEN DAFFODILS BEGIN TO PEER
by *William Shakespeare (1564-1616)*

When daffodils begin to peer,
    With heigh! the doxy over the dale,
Why, then comes in the sweet o' the year;
    For the red blood reigns in the winter's pale.

The white sheet bleaching on the hedge,
    With heigh! the sweet birds, oh, how they sing!
Doth set my pugging tooth on edge;
    For a quart of ale is a dish for a king.

The lark, that tirra-lirra chaunts,
    With heigh! with heigh! the thrush and the jay,
Are summer songs for me and my aunts
    While we lie tumbling in the hay.

from LONDON THEATRES
by *Thomas Bellamy (1745-c.1800)*

In Drury's widen'd amphitheatre
In scenes like these, where sound must be conveyed
To the far distant crown in gallery rows,
Propriety is outraged. Those below
(Plac'd at just distance, in the neighbouring pit)
Behold the Roman traitor steal toward
The couch of sleeping gentle Imogen,
As fearful every step might wake the fair.
Behold him view the chamber, and, at length,
Note on her bosom the 'cinque spotted' mole:
Then, hear him tell his villainous intent,
In tones high rais'd, discordant, and unfit,
To gods assembled in their lofty seats!

Drury, thy vast and tow'ring space has prov'd
The builder's triumph, but the actor's bane.
On thy broad boards, the whistling winds around
Annoy the shiv'ring hero, as he moves
And chatters o'er his lesson, numb'd by cold
Intense, and hurtful to his powers and frame.
Triumph ye dancing and ye dumb-show tribe,
Where the light heel, a stranger to the head,
Hath now brave footing for its mazy rounds.
Ye bulls, ye bears, rejoice! Ye chargers, thrive,
Thrive in your stalls theatric, pamper'd high,
For grand and glittering spectacles to come.

from THE EXCURSION

by *William Wordsworth (1770-1850)*

A single step, that freed me from the skirts
Of the blind vapour, opened to my view
Glory beyond all glory ever seen
By waking sense or by the dreaming soul!
The appearance, instantaneously disclosed,
Was of a mighty city – boldly say
A wilderness of building, sinking far
And self-withdrawn into a boundless depth,
Far sinking into splendour – without end!

Fabric it seemed of diamond and of gold,
With alabaster domes, and silver spires,
And blazing terrace upon terrace, high
Uplifted; here, serene pavilions bright,
In avenues disposed; there, towers begirt
With battlements that on their restless fronts
Bore stars – illumination of all gems!
By earthly nature had the effect been wrought
Upon the dark materials of the storm
Now pacified; on them, and on the coves
And mountain-steeps and summits, whereunto
The vapours had receded, taking there
Their station under a cerulean sky.
Oh, 'twas an unimaginable sight!

from ULYSSES

by *Alfred, Lord Tennyson (1809-1892)*

It little profits that an idle king,
By this still hearth, among these barren crags,
Matched with an aged wife, I mete and dole
Unequal laws unto a savage race,
That hoard, and sleep, and feed, and know not me.
I cannot rest from travel: I will drink
Life to the lees: all times I have enjoyed
Greatly, have suffered greatly, both with those
That loved me, and alone; on shore, and when
Thro' scudding drifts the rainy Hyades
Vext the dim sea. I am become a name:
For always roaming with a hungry heart
Much have I seen and known: cities of men
And manners, climates, councils, governments,
Myself not least, but honoured of them all;
And drunk delight of battle with my peers,
Far on the ringing plains of windy Troy.
I am a part of all that I have met;
Yet all experience is an arch wherethro'
Gleams that untravelled world, whose margin fades
For ever and for ever when I move.
How dull it is to pause, to make an end,
To rust unburnished, not to shine in use!
As tho' to breathe were life.

from CHRONICLES
by *Raphael Holinshed (c.1529-c.1580)*

It fortuned as Makbeth and Banquho journeyed towards Fores, where the king then lay, they went sporting by the way together without other company save only themselves, passing through the woods and fields, when suddenly in the middest of a laund, there met them three women in strange and wild apparel, resembling creatures of the elder world, whom when they attentively beheld, wondering much at the sight, the first of them spake and said: 'All hail, Makbeth, thane of Glammis!' (for he had lately entered into that office by the death of his father Sinell). The second of them said: 'Hail Makbeth, thane of Cawdor!' But the third said: 'All hail Makbeth, that hereafter shall be king of Scotland!'

Then Banquho: 'What manner of women (saith he) are you that seem so little favourable unto me, whereas to my fellow here, besides high offices, ye assign also the kingdom, appointing forth nothing for me at all?' 'Yes,' (saith the first of them,) 'we promise greater benefits unto thee than unto him; for he shall reign indeed, but with an unlucky end; neither shall he leave any issue behind him to succeed in his place, when certainly thou shalt not reign at all, but of thee those shall be born which shall govern the Scottish kingdom by long order of continual descent.' Herewith the foresaid women vanished immediately out of their sight. This was reputed at the first but some vain fantastical illusion by Makbeth and Banquho, insomuch that Banquho would call Makbeth in jest, King of Scotland; and Makbeth again would call him in sport likewise, father of many kings. But afterwards the common opinion was, that these women were either the weird sisters, that is (as ye would say) the goddesses of destiny, or else some nymphs or fairies, indued with knowledge of prophecie by their necromantical science, because everything came to pass as they had spoken.

from THE STORY OF GILETTA OF NARBONA

by *William Painter (c.1540-1594)*

And then she repaired to the King, praying his grace to vouchsafe to show her his disease.

The King, perceiving her to be a fair young maiden and a comely, would not hide it, but opened the same unto her. So soon as she saw it she put him in comfort, that she was able to heal him, saying:

'Sire, if it shall please your grace, I trust in God, without any pain or grief unto your highness, within eight days I will make you whole of this disease.'

The King, hearing her say so, began to mock her, saying:

'How is it possible for thee, being a young woman, to do that which the best renowned physicians in the world can not?' He thanked her for her good will and made her a direct answer that he was determined no more to follow the counsel of any physician. Where-unto the maiden answered:

'Sire, you despise my knowledge because I am young and a woman. But I assure you that I do not minister physic by profession but by the aid and help of God, and with the cunning of Master Gerardo of Narbona, who was my father, and a physician of great fame so long as he lived.'

The King, hearing those words, said to himself: 'This woman, peradventure, is sent unto me of God; and therefore why should I disdain to prove her cunning? sithence she promiseth to heal me within a little space, without any offence or grief unto me.' And being determined to prove her, he said:

'Damosel, if thou dost not heal me, but make me to break my determination, what wilt thou shall follow thereof?'

'Sire,' said the maiden, 'let me be kept in what guard and keeping you list. And if I do not heal you within these eight days, let me be burnt. But if I do heal your grace, what recompense shall I have then?'

To whom the King answered:

'Because thou art a maiden and unmarried, if thou heal me according to thy promise, I will bestow thee upon some gentleman that shall be of right good worship and estimation.'

73

from THE STORY OF APOLONIUS AND SILLA

by *Barnaby Rich (c.1540-1617)*

Gentlewomen, according to my promise, I will here, for brevity's sake, omit to make repetition of the long and dolorous discourse recorded by Silla for this sudden departure of her Apolonius, knowing you to be as tenderly-hearted as Silla herself; whereby you may the better conjecture the fury of her fever.

But Silla, the further that she saw herself bereaved of all hope ever any more to see her beloved Apolonius, so much the more contagious were her passions, and made the greater speed to execute that she had premeditated in her mind; which was this – amongst many servants that did attend upon her, there was one whose name was Pedro, who had a long time waited upon her in her chamber; whereby she was well assured of his fidelity and trust. To that Pedro therefore she bewrayed first the fervency of her love borne to Apolonius, conjuring him in the name of the goddess of love herself and binding him by the duty that a servant ought to have, that tendereth his mistress's safety and good liking, and desiring him with tears trickling down her cheeks that he would give his consent to aid and assist her in that she had determined; which was (for that she was fully resolved to go to Constantinople where she might again take the view of her beloved Apolonius) that he, according to the trust she had reposed in him, would not refuse to give his consent secretly to convey her from out her father's court according as she should give him direction; and also to make himself partaker of her journey, and to wait upon her, till she had seen the end of her determination.

from SIR SIMON EYER

by *Thomas Deloney (1543-1607)*

How Simon Eyer was sent for to my Lord Maiors to supper, and shewing the great entertainment he and his wife had there.

Anon, after supper time drew neer, she, making herselfe ready in the best manner she could deuise, passed along with her husband vnto my Lord Maiors hovse: and being entred into the great hall, one of the officers there certified my Lord Maior, that the great, rich shoomaker and his wife were already come. Whereupon the Lord Maior in courteous manner came into the hall to Simon, saying, You are most heartily welcome good Master Eyer, and so is your gentle bed-fellow. Then came forth the Lady Maiores and saluted them both in like manner, saying, Welcome, good Master Eyer and Mistresse Eyer both: and taking her by the hand, set her down among the gentlewomen there present.

Sir (quoth the Lord Maior) I vnderstand you are a shoomaker, and that it is you that hath bought up all the goods of the great Argozy.

I am indeed, my lord of the Gentle craft (quoth he) and I praise God, all the goods of the great Argozy are mine own, when my debts are paid.

God giue you much ioy of them (said the Lord Maior) and I trust you and I shall deal for some part thereof.

So the meat being then ready to be brought in, the guests were placed each one according to their calling. My Lord Maior holding Simon by the hand, and the Lady Maiores holding his wife, they would needs haue them sit neer to themselues, which they then with blushing cheeks refusing, my lord said vnto them, holding his cap in his hand.

Master Eyer and Mistresse Eyer, let me intreat you not to be troublesome, for I tell you it shall be thus: and as for those gentlemen here present, they are all of mine old acquaintance, and many times we haue been together, therefore I dare be the bolder with them: albeit you are our neighbours also, yet I promise you, you are strangers to my table, and to strangers common courtesie doth teach vs to shew the greatest fauour, and therefore let me rule you in mine house, and you shall rule me in yours.

from ARDEN OF FAVERSHAM

Anon. 1592

MICHAEL: He is and fain would have the light away.
Conflicting thoughts encamped in my breast
Awake me with the echo of their strokes;
And I, a judge to censure either side,
Can give to neither wished victory.
My master's kindness pleads to me for life
With just demand, and I must grant it him;
My mistress, she hath forced me with an oath,
For Susan's sake, the which I may not break,
For that is nearer than a master's love;
That grim-faced fellow, pitiless Black Will,
And Shakebag, stern in bloody stratagem –
Two rougher ruffians never lived in Kent –
Have sworn my death if I infringe my vow,
A dreadful thing to be consider'd of.
Methinks I see them with their bolter'd hair,
Staring and grinning in thy gentle face,
And in their ruthless hands their daggers drawn,
Insulting o'er thee with a peck of oaths,
Whilst thou, submissive, pleading for relief,
Art mangled by their ireful instruments.
Methinks I hear them ask where Michael is,
And pitiless Black Will cries 'Stab the slave!
The peasant will detect the tragedy.'
The wrinkles in his foul, death-threat'ning face
Gapes open wide, like graves to swallow men.
My death to him is but a merriment,
And he will murder me to make him sport.
He comes, he comes! Ah, Master Franklin, help!
Call up the neighbours or we are but dead!

from EDWARD III

Anon. 1596, attributed to William Shakespeare

COUNTESS OF SALISBURY:

But that your lips were sacred, my lord,

You would profane the holy name of love.

That love, you offer me, you cannot give,

For Caesar owes that tribute to his queen:

That love, you beg of me, I cannot give,

For Sara owes that duty to her lord.

He that doth clip or counterfeit your stamp

Shall die, my lord: and will your sacred self

Commit high treason against the King of Heaven,

To stamp his image in forbidden metal,

Forgetting your allegiance and your oath?

In violating marriage' sacred law,

You break a greater honour than yourself:

To be a king, is of a younger house

Than to be married: your progenitor,

Sole-reigning Adam on the universe,

By God was honour'd for a married man,

But not by him anointed for a king.

It is a penalty to break your statutes,

Though not enacted with your highness' hand:

How much more, to infringe the holy act

Made by the mouth of God, seal'd with his hand?

I know, my sovereign – in my husband's love,

Who now doth loyal service in his wars –

Doth but to try the wife of Salisbury,

Whether she will hear a wanton's tale, or no;

Lest being therein guilty by my stay,

From that, not from my liege, I turn away.

from THE PURITAINE

Anon. 1607

PIEBOARD (*to the audience*):

So all this comes well about yet: I play the fortune-teller as well as if I had had a witch to my grannam. For by good happiness, being in my hostess's garden, which neighbours the orchard of the widow, I laid the hole of mine ear to a hole in the wall, and heard 'em make these vows and speak those words upon which I wrought these advantages: and to encourage my forgery the more, I may now perceive in 'em a natural simplicity which will easily swallow an abuse, if any covering be over it.

And to confirm my former presage to the widow, I have advised old Peter Skirmish, the soldier, to hurt Corporal Oath upon the leg; and in that hurry I'll rush amongst 'em; and instead of giving the Corporal some cordial to comfort him, I'll pour into his mouth a potion of a sleepy nature, to make him seem as dead. For the which the old soldier being apprehended, and ready to be borne to execution, I'll step in, and take upon me the cure of the dead man, upon pain of dying the condemned's death: the Corporal will wake at his minute, when the sleepy force has wrought itself, and so shall I get myself into a most admired opinion, and under the pretext of that cunning, beguile as I see occasion. And if that foolish Nicholas Saint-Tantlings keep true time with the chain, my plot will be sound, the Captain delivered, and my wits applauded among scholars and soldiers for ever.

from AS YOU LIKE IT

by *William Shakespeare (1564-1616)*

ROSALIND:

I will weary you then no longer with idle talking. Know of me then, for now I speak to some purpose, that I know you are a gentleman of good conceit. I speak not this that you should bear a good opinion of my knowledge, insomuch I say I know you are; neither do I labour for a greater esteem than may in some little measure draw a belief from you to do yourself good, and not to grace me. Believe then, if you please, that I can do strange things: I have, since I was three year old, conversed with a magician, most profound in his art, and yet not damnable. If you do love Rosalind so near the heart as your gesture cries it out, when your brother marries Aliena, shall you marry her. I know into what straits of fortune she is driven, and it is not impossible to me, if it appear not inconvenient to you, to set her before your eyes tomorrow, human as she is, and without any danger. . .

Therefore, put you in your best array, bid your friends; for if you will be married tomorrow, you shall; and to Rosalind, if you will.

from A YORKSHIRE TRAGEDY

Anon. 1608

WIFE: What will become of us? All will away;
        My husband never ceases in expense,
        Both to consume his credit and his house;
        And 'tis set down by Heaven's just decree
        That riot's child must needs be beggary.
        Are these the virtues that his youth did promise,
        Dice, and voluptuous meetings, midnight revels,
        Taking his bed with surfeits? – ill beseeming
        The ancient honour of his house and name.
        And this not all, but that which kills me most,
        When he recounts his losses and false fortunes,
        The weakness of his state so much dejected,
        Not as a man repentant, but half mad
        His fortunes cannot answer his expense.
        He sits and sullenly locks up his arms;
        Forgetting Heaven, looks downward, which makes him
        Appear so dreadful that he frights my heart;
        Walks heavily, as if his soul were earth;
        Not penitent for those his sins are past,
        But vext his money cannot make them last:
        A fearful melancholy, ungodly sorrow.
        Oh, yonder he comes. Now in despite of ills
        I'll speak to him, and I will hear him speak,
        And do my best to drive it from his heart.

from PERICLES

by *William Shakespeare (1564-1616)*

PERICLES: Thou speak'st like a physician, Helicanus,

That ministers a potion unto me

That thou wouldst tremble to receive thyself.

Attend me then: I went to Antioch,

Where, as thou know'st, against the face of death

I sought the purchase of a glorious beauty,

From whence an issue I might propagate

Are arms to princes and bring joys to subjects.

Her face was to mine eye beyond all wonder;

The rest – hark in thine ear – as black as incest;

Which by my knowledge found, the sinful father

Seemed not to strike, but smooth; but thou know'st this:

'Tis time to fear when tyrants seem to kiss.

Which fear so grew in me, I hither fled,

Under the covering of a careful night,

Who seemed my good protector; and, being here,

Bethought me what was past, what might succeed.

I knew him tyrannous; and tyrants' fears

Decrease not, but grow faster than the years;

And should he doubt, as no doubt he doth,

That I should open to the list'ning air

How many worthy princes' bloods were shed

To keep his bed of blackness unlaid ope,

To lop that doubt, he'll fill this land with arms,

And make pretense of wrong that I have done him;

When all for mine, if I may call, offense

Must feel war's blow, who spares not innocence;

Which love to all, of which thyself art one,

Who now reprovedst me for't –

from THE SHOEMAKER'S HOLIDAY

by *Thomas Dekker (c.1570-1632)*

LACY: How many shapes have gods and kings devised
       Thereby to compass their desirèd loves?
       It is no shame for Rowland Lacy, then,
       To clothe his cunning with the Gentle Craft,
       That thus disguised I may unknown possess
       The only happy presence of my Rose.
       For her I have forsook my charge in France,
       Incurred the King's displeasure, and stirred up
       Rough hatred in mine uncle Lincoln's breast.
       Oh love, how powerful art thou, that canst change
       High birth to bareness, and a noble mind
       To the mean semblance of a shoemaker!
       But thus it must be: for her cruel father,
       Hating the single union of our souls,
       Hath secretly conveyed my Rose from London,
       To bar me of her presence. But I trust
       Fortune and this disguise will further me
       Once more to view her beauty, gain her sight.
       Here in Tower Street, with Eyre the shoemaker,
       Mean I awhile to work. I know the trade,
       I learnt it when I was in Wittenberg.
       Then cheer thy hoping spirits, be not dismayed:
       Thou canst not want, do Fortune what she can.
       The Gentle Craft is living for a man.

from THE NEW INN

by *Ben Jonson (1572-1637)*

LADY FRAMPUL: What penance shall I do to be received,
              And reconciled to the church of Love?
              Go on procession, barefoot, to his image,
              And say some hundred penitential verses,
              There, out of Chaucer's Troilus and Cressid?
              Or to his mother's shrine, vow a wax-candle
              As large as the town May-pole is, and pay it?
              Enjoin me any thing this court thinks fit,
              For I have trespass'd, and blasphemed Love:
              I have, indeed, despised his deity,
              Whom (till this miracle wrought on me) I knew not.
              Now I adore Love, and would kiss the rushes
              That bear this reverend gentleman, his priest,
              If that would expiate – but I fear it will not.
              For, though he be somewhat struck in years, and old
              Enough to be my father, he is wise,
              And only wise men love, the other covet.
              I could begin to be in love with him,
              But will not tell him yet, because I hope
              To enjoy the other hour with more delight,
              And prove him farther.
              [. . .]
              How swift is time, and slily steals away
              From them would hug it, value it, embrace it!
              I should have thought it scarce had run ten minutes,
              When the whole hour is fled. Here, take your kiss, sir,
              Which I most willingly tender you in court.

GRADE 8

CLOCK-O'-CLAY
by *John Clare (1793-1864)*

In the cowslip pips I lie,
Hidden from the buzzing fly,
While green grass beneath me lies,
Pearled with dew like fishes' eyes,
Here I lie, a clock-o'-clay,
Waiting for the time o' day.

While the forest quakes surprise,
And the wild wind sobs and sighs,
My home rocks as like to fall,
On its pillar green and tall;
When the pattering rain drives by
Clock-o'-clay keeps warm and dry.

Day by day and night by night,
All the week I hide from sight;
In the cowslip pips I lie,
In the rain still warm and dry;
Day and night, and night and day,
Red, black-spotted clock-o'-clay.

My home shakes in wind and showers,
Pale green pillar topped with flowers,
Bending at the wild wind's breath,
Till I touch the grass beneath;
Here I live, lone clock-o'-clay,
Watching for the time of day.

PROSPICE

by *Robert Browning (1812-1889)*

Fear death? – to feel the fog in my throat,
    The mist in my face,
When the snows begin, and the blasts denote
    I am nearing the place,
The power of the night, the press of the storm,
    The post of the foe;
Where he stands, the Arch Fear in a visible form,
    Yet the strong man must go:
For the journey is done and the summit attained,
    And the barriers fall,
Though a battle's to fight ere the guerdon be gained,
    The reward of it all.
I was ever a fighter, so – one fight more,
    The best and the last!
I would hate that death bandaged my eyes, and forbore,
    And bade me creep past,
No! let me taste the whole of it, fare like my peers
    The heroes of old,
Bear the brunt, in a minute pay glad life's arrears
    Of pain, darkness and cold.
For sudden the worst turns the best to the brave,
    The black minute's at end,
And the elements' rage, the fiend-voices that rave,
    Shall dwindle, shall blend,
Shall change, shall become first a peace out of pain,
    Then a light, then thy breast,
O thou soul of my soul! I shall clasp thee again,
    And with God be the rest!

JABBERWOCKY

by *Lewis Carroll (1832-1898)*

'Twas brillig, and the slithy toves
  Did gyre and gimble in the wabe:
All mimsy were the borogoves,
  And the mome raths outgrabe.

'Beware the Jabberwock, my son!
  The jaws that bite, the claws that catch!
Beware the Jubjub bird, and shun
  The frumious Bandersnatch!'

He took his vorpal sword in hand;
  Long time the manxome foe he sought–
So rested he by the Tumtum tree,
  And stood awhile in thought.

And, as in uffish thought he stood,
  The Jabberwock, with eyes of flame,
Came whiffling through the tulgey wood,
  And burbled as it came!

One, two! One, two! And through and through
  The vorpal blade went snicker-snack!
He left it dead, and with its head
  He went galumphing back.

'And hast thou slain the Jabberwock?
  Come to my arms, my beamish boy!
O frabjous day! Callooh, Callay!'
  He chortled in his joy.

'Twas brillig, and the slithy toves
  Did gyre and gimble in the wabe:
All mimsy were the borogoves,
  And the mome raths outgrabe.

ALL THESE . . .
by *Peter Ackroyd (1949-)*

all these particles of knowledge
are a stick which I carry in my hand
pulled out of the vast emptiness
of a day at the sea

I looked up into the branches
and I saw nothing
except the wind
and its persistent insect

the dunes incline towards me
and the noisome truth
is the knowledge
that you will have to leave this place

the branch floating down
haunted by itself
as a body
having to change what it loves

by *Gerard Manley Hopkins (1844-1889)*

As kingfishers catch fire, dragonflies draw flame;
   As tumbled over rim in roundy wells
   Stones ring; like each tucked string tells, each hung bell's
Bow swung finds tongue to fling out broad its name;
Each mortal thing does one thing and the same:
   Deals out that being indoors each one dwells;
   Selves – goes its self; *myself* it speaks and spells,
Crying *What I do is me: for that I came.*

I say more: the just man justices;
   Keeps grace: that keeps all his goings graces;
Acts in God's eye what in God's eye he is –
   Christ. For Christ plays in ten thousand places,
Lovely in limbs, and lovely in eyes not his
   To the Father through the features of men's faces.

THE WAYFARER

by *Patrick Pearse (1879-1916)*

Written the night before his execution

The beauty of the world hath made me sad,
This beauty that will pass;
Sometimes my heart hath shaken with great joy
To see a leaping squirrel in a tree,
Or a red ladybird upon a stalk,
Or little rabbits in a field at evening,
Lit by a slanting sun,
Or some green hill where shadows drifted by,
Some quiet hill where mountainy man hath sown
And soon would reap; near to the gate of heaven;
Or children with bare feet upon the sands
Of some ebbed sea, or playing on the streets
Of little towns in Connacht,
Things young and happy.
And then my heart hath told me:
These will pass,
Will pass and change, will die and be no more,
Things bright and green, things young and happy;
And I have gone upon my way
Sorrowful.

ATLAS

by *U. A. Fanthorpe (1929-)*

There is a kind of love called maintenance,
Which stores the WD40 and knows when to use it;

Which checks the insurance, and doesn't forget
The milkman; which remembers to plant bulbs;

Which answers letters; which knows the way
The money goes; which deals with dentists

And Road Fund Tax and meeting trains,
And postcards to the lonely; which upholds

The permanently ricketty elaborate
Structures of living; which is Atlas.

And maintenance is the sensible side of love,
Which knows what time and weather are doing
To my brickwork; insulates my faulty wiring;
Laughs at my dryrotten jokes; remembers
My need for gloss and grouting; which keeps
My suspect edifice upright in air,
As Atlas did the sky.

BAVARIAN GENTIANS

by *D. H. Lawrence (1885-1930)*

Not every man has gentians in his house
in Soft September, at slow, sad Michaelmas.

Bavarian gentians, big and dark, only dark
darkening the day-time, torch-like with the smoking blueness of Pluto's
    gloom,
ribbed and torch-like, with their blaze of darkness spread blue
down flattening into points, flattened under the sweep of white day
torch-flower of the blue-smoking darkness, Pluto's dark-blue daze,
black lamps from the halls of Dis, burning dark blue,
giving off darkness, blue darkness, as Demeter's pale lamps give off light,
lead me then, lead the way.

Reach me a gentian, give me a torch!
let me guide myself with the blue, forked torch of this flower
down the darker and darker stairs, where blue is darkened on blueness
even where Persephone goes, just now, from the frosted September
to the sightless realm where darkness is awake upon the dark
and Persephone herself is but a voice
or a darkness invisible enfolded in the deeper dark
of the arms Plutonic, and pierced with the passion of dense gloom,
among the splendour of torches of darkness, shedding darkness on the lost
    bride and her groom.

from EMMA

by *Jane Austen (1775-1817)*

'How much I am obliged to you,' said he, 'for telling me to come to-day! – If it had not been for you, I should certainly have lost all the happiness of this party. I had quite determined to go away again.'

'Yes, you were very cross; and I do not know what about, except that you were too late for the best strawberries. I was a kinder friend than you deserved. But you were humble. You begged hard to be commanded to come.'

'Don't say I was cross. I was fatigued. The heat overcame me.'

'It is hotter to-day.'

'Not to my feelings. I am perfectly comfortable to-day.'

'You are comfortable because you are under command.'

'Your command? – Yes.'

'Perhaps I intended you to say so, but I meant self-command. You had, somehow or other, broken bounds yesterday, and run away from your own management; but to-day you are got back again – and as I cannot be always with you, it is best to believe your temper under your own command rather than mine.'

'It comes to the same thing. I can have no self-command without a motive. You order me, whether you speak or not. And you can be always with me. You are always with me.'

'Dating from three o'clock yesterday. My perpetual influence could not begin earlier, or you would not have been so much out of humour before.'

'Three o'clock yesterday! That is your date. I thought I had seen you first in February.'

'Your gallantry is really unanswerable. But (lowering her voice) – nobody speaks except ourselves, and it is rather too much to be talking nonsense for the entertainment of seven silent people.'

'I say nothing of which I am ashamed,' replied he, with lively impudence. 'I saw you first in February. Let everybody on the Hill hear me if they can. Let my accents swell to Mickleham on one side, and Dorking on the other. I saw you first in February.' And then whispering – 'Our companions are exceedingly stupid. What shall we do to rouse them? Any nonsense will serve. They *shall* talk. Ladies and gentlemen, I am ordered by Miss Woodhouse (who, wherever she is, presides,) to say, that she desires to know what you are all thinking of?'

Some laughed, and answered good-humouredly. Miss Bates said a great deal; Mrs Elton swelled at the idea of Miss Woodhouse's presiding; Mr Knightley's answer was the most distinct.

from SQUIRE TOBY'S WILL

by *J. Sheridan Le Fanu (1814-1873)*

I don't think, with the exception of old Cooper, that the servants cared for this prohibition, except as it baulked a curiosity always strong in the solitude of the country. Cooper was very much vexed that the eldest son of the old Squire should be buried in the old family chapel, and no sign of decent respect from Gylingden Hall. He asked his master, whether he would not, at least, have some wine and refreshments in the oak parlour, in case any of the country gentlemen who paid this respect to the old family should come up to the house? But the Squire only swore at him, told him to mind his own business, and ordered him to say, if such a thing happened, that he was out, and no preparations made, and, in fact, to send them away as they came. Cooper expostulated stoutly, and the Squire grew angrier; and after a tempestuous scene, took his hat and stick and walked out, just as the funeral descending the valley from the direction of the 'Old Angel Inn' came in sight.

Old Cooper prowled about disconsolately, and counted the carriages as well as he could from the gate. When the funeral was over, and they began to drive away, he returned to the hall, the door of which lay open, and as usual deserted. Before he reached it quite, a mourning coach drove up, and two gentlemen in black cloaks, and crapes to their hats, got out, and without looking to the right or the left, went up the steps into the house. Cooper followed them slowly. The carriage had, he supposed, gone round to the yard, for, when he reached the door, it was no longer there.

So he followed the two mourners into the house. In the hall he found a fellow-servant, who said he had seen two gentlemen, in black cloaks, pass through the hall, and go up the stairs without removing their hats, or asking leave of anyone. This was very odd, old Cooper thought, and a great liberty; so upstairs he went to make them out.

But he could not find them then, nor ever. And from that hour the house was troubled.

from THROUGH THE LOOKING GLASS

by *Lewis Carroll (1832-1898)*

'Tickets, please!' said the Guard, putting his head in at the window. In a moment everybody was holding out a ticket: they were about the same size as the people, and quite seemed to fill the carriage.

'Now then! Show your ticket, child!' the Guard went on, looking angrily at Alice. And a great many voices all said together ('like the chorus of the song,' thought Alice), 'Don't keep him waiting, child! Why, his time is worth a thousand pounds a minute!'

'I'm afraid I haven't got one,' Alice said in a frightened tone: 'there wasn't a ticket-office where I came from.' And again the chorus of voices went on: 'There wasn't room for one where she came from. The land there is worth a thousand pounds an inch!'

'Don't make excuses,' said the Guard: 'you should have bought one from the engine-driver.' And once more the chorus of voices went on with 'The man that drives the engine. Why, the smoke alone is worth a thousand pounds a puff!'

Alice thought to herself, 'Then there's no use in speaking.' The voices didn't join in this time, as she hadn't spoken, but, to her great surprise, they all *thought* in chorus (I hope you understand what *thinking in chorus* means – for I must confess that *I* don't), 'Better say nothing at all. Language is worth a thousand pounds a word!'

'I shall dream about a thousand pounds to-night, I know I shall!' thought Alice.

All this time the Guard was looking at her, first through a telescope, then through a microscope, and then through an opera-glass. At last he said, 'You're travelling the wrong way,' and shut up the window and went away.

from THE CRITIC AS ARTIST

by *Oscar Wilde (1854-1900)*

GILBERT: Yes; the critic will be an interpreter, if he chooses. He can pass from his synthetic impression of the work of art as a whole, to an analysis or exposition of the work itself, and in this lower sphere, as I hold it to be, there are many delightful things to be said and done. Yet his object will not always be to explain the work of art. He may seek rather to deepen its mystery, to raise round it, and round its maker, that mist of wonder which is dear to both gods and worshippers alike. Ordinary people are 'terribly at ease in Zion.' They propose to walk arm in arm with the poets, and have a glib ignorant way of saying, 'Why should we read what is written about Shakespeare and Milton? We can read the plays and the poems. That is enough.' But an appreciation of Milton is, as the late Rector of Lincoln remarked once, the reward of consummate scholarship. And he who desires to understand Shakespeare truly must understand the relations in which Shakespeare stood to the Renaissance and the Reformation, to the age of Elizabeth and the age of James: he must be familiar with the history of the struggle for supremacy between the old classical forms and the new spirit of romance, between the school of Sidney, and Daniel, and Johnson, and the school of Marlowe and Marlowe's greater son; he must know the materials that were at Shakespeare's disposal, and the method in which he used them, and the conditions of theatric presentation in the sixteenth and seventeenth century, their limitations and their opportunities for freedom, and the literary criticism of Shakespeare's day, its aims and modes and canons; he must study the English language in its progress, and blank or rhymed verse in its various developments; he must study the Greek drama, and the connection between the art of the creator of the Agamemnon and the art of the creator of Macbeth; in a word, he must be able to bind Elizabethan London to the Athens of Pericles, and to learn Shakespeare's true position in the history of European drama and the drama of the world.

from THE GARRICK FEVER

by *James Robinson Planché (1796-1880)*

GINGLE: (*looking about him*)

'Thus far into the bowels of the land have we march'd on without impediment.' They said the manager was in his room: 'There's no such thing!' Well, I must sit down, at all events, for I'm tired to death! Five and twenty miles have I walked this blessed day, and without eating since my breakfast. (*Takes out a play-bill.*) The sight of this bill, however, as I entered the town, gave me fresh spirits. Garrick is here! – the great unrivalled Garrick! If I could but get an engagement – were it only to carry a letter, or deliver a message; anything by which I might meet the eye of the great Roscius, and, perhaps, obtain his approbation and patronage – who knows what might happen? – He might take me with him to London – get me an appearance at Drury Lane – fancy our names in the same bill – 'Duke of Gloster, Mr Garrick. The Lord Mayor, Mr Gingle, from the Theatre Royal, Ballinaslough (being his first appearance in London).' Oh, ambition! 'By that sin, fell the angels'! I can't help it. I feel, somehow, I shall be somebody, some day or another.

'Swift it mounts on eagles' wings;

Kings it makes gods, and meaner creatures kings.'

There must be a chance for me, here. (*looking at the bill*) They seem horribly off for members, and the whole family is pressed into the service. (*Reads:*) 'Ghost, Mr Hardup – Ophelia, Miss Polly Hardup – and Polonius and Osrick, doubled by Mr Terence Hardup.' They're all Hardup! If they'd let me play Osrick, now, I might make – 'a hit, my lord – a palpable hit'! Somebody comes – should it be the manager!

'Hold, hold, my heart –

And you, my sinews, grow not instant old,

But bear me stiffly up!' (*Retires*)

from THE LAMPLIGHTER

by *Charles Dickens (1812-1870)*

TOM: Well, that's the queerest genius I ever came across, – rather a singular person for a little smoking party. (*Looks into the crucible.*) This is the saucepan, I suppose, where they're boiling the philosopher's stone down to the proper consistency. I hope it's nearly done; when it's quite ready, I'll send out for six-penn'orth of sprats, and turn 'em into gold fish for a first experiment. 'Cod! it'll be a comfortable thing though to have no end to one's riches. I'll have a country house and a park, and I'll plant a bit of it with a double row of gas-lamps a mile long, and go out with a French polished mahogany ladder, and two servants in livery behind me, to light 'em with my own hands every night. What's to be seen here? (*Looks through telescope.*) Nothing particular, the stopper being on at the other end. The little boy with three heads (*looking towards the case*). What a comfort he must have been to his parents! – Halloa! (*taking up a large knife*) this is a disagreeable looking instrument, – something too large for bread and cheese, or oysters, and not of a bad shape for sticking live persons in the ribs. A very dismal place this, – I wish they'd come back. Ah! – (*coming upon the skeleton*) here's a ghastly object, – what does the writing say? – (*reads a label upon the case*) 'Skeleton of a gentleman prepared by Mr Mooney.' I hope Mr Mooney may not be in the habit of inviting gentlemen here, and making 'em into such preparations without their own consent. Here's a book, now. What's all this about, I wonder? The letters look as if a steam-engine had printed 'em by accident. (*Turns over the leaves, spelling to himself.*)

from THE TICKET-OF-LEAVE MAN

by *Tom Taylor (1817-1880)*

MAY: There, Goldie, I must give *you* your breakfast, though I don't care a bit for my own. Ah! you find singing a better trade than I did, you little rogue. I'm sure I shall have a letter from Robert this morning. I've all his letters here (*taking out a packet from her work-box*). How he has improved in his handwriting since the first. (*opening letter.*) That's more than three years back. Oh! what an old woman I'm getting! It's no use denying it, Goldie. (*to her bird.*) If you'll be quiet, like a good, well-bred canary, I'll read you Robert's last letter. (*Reads:*) 'Portland, February 25th, 1860. My own dearest May, – (*kissing it.*) As the last year keeps slipping away, I think more and more of our happy meeting; but for your love and comfort I think I should have broken down.' Goldie, do you hear that? (*She kisses the letter.*) 'But now we both see how things are guided for the best. But for my being sent to prison, I should have died before this, a broken-down drunkard, if not worse; and you might still have been earning hard bread as a street-singer, or carried from a hospital ward to a pauper's grave.' Yes, yes, (*shuddering*) that's true. 'This place has made a man of me, and you have found friends and the means of earning a livelihood. I count the days till we meet. Good-bye and heaven bless you, prays your ever affectionate Robert Brierly.' (*Kisses the letter frequently.*) And don't I count the days too? There! (*Makes a mark in her pocket almanack.*) Another gone! They seem so slow – when one looks forward – and yet they pass so quickly! (*Taking up birdcage.*) Come, Goldie, while I work you must sing me a nice song for letting you hear that nice letter. (*Hanging up birdcage – a knock at the door.*)

from CASTE

by *T. W. Robertson (1829-1871)*

ECCLES: Poor Esther! Nice market she's brought her pigs to – ugh! Mind the baby indeed! What good is he to me? That fool of a girl to throw away all her chances! – a *honourable-hess* – and her father not to have on him the price of a pint of early beer or a quartern of cool, refreshing gin! Stopping in here to rock a young honourable! Cuss him! Are we slaves, we working men? (*Sings:*)

'Britons never, never, never shall be —'

I won't stand this, I've writ to the old cat – I mean to the Marquissy – to tell her that her daughter-in-law and her grandson is almost starving. That fool Esther's too proud to write to her for money. I hate pride – it's *beastly*! There's no beastly pride about me. I'm as dry as a lime-kiln. (*Takes up jug.*) Milk! – (*with disgust*) – for this young aristocratic pauper. Everybody in the house is sacrificed for him! And to think that a *working man*, and a member of the Committee of the Banded Brothers for the Regeneration of Human Kind, by means of equal diffusion of intelligence and equal division of property, should be thusty, while this cub – (*Draws aside curtain, and looks at child. After a pause:*) That there coral he's got round his neck is *gold*, real *gold*! Oh, Society! Oh, Governments! Oh, Class Legislation! – *is this right*? Shall this mindless wretch enjoy himself, while sleeping, with a jewelled gawd, and his poor old grandfather want the price of half a pint? *No*! it shall not be! Rather than see it, I will myself resent this outrage on the rights of man! and in this holy crusade of class against class, of the weak and lowly against the *powerful and strong* – (*pointing to child*) – I will strike one blow for freedom! (*Goes to back of cradle.*) He's asleep. It will fetch ten bob round the corner; and if the Marquissy gives us anythink it can be got out with some o' that. (*Steals coral.*) Lie still, my darling! – it's grandfather's a-watching over you –

'Who ran to catch me when I fell,

And kicked the place to make it well?

My grandfather!'

from PYGMALION AND GALATEA

by *W. S. Gilbert (1836-1911)*

GALATEA: And then I sat alone and wept – and wept

A long, long time for my Pygmalion.

Then by degrees – by tedious degrees,

The light – the glorious light! – the God-sent light –

I saw it sink – sink – sink – behind the world!

Then I grew cold – cold – as I used to be,

Before my loved Pygmalion gave me life,

Then came the fearful thought that, by degrees,

I was returning into stone again!

How bitterly I wept and prayed aloud

That it might not be so! 'Spare me, ye gods!

Spare me,' I cried, 'for my Pygmalion,

A little longer for Pygmalion!

Oh, take me not so early from my love;

Oh, let me see him once – but once again!'

But no – they heard me not, for they are good,

And had they heard, must needs have pitied me;

They had not seen *thee*, and they did not know

The happiness that I must leave behind.

I fell upon thy couch, my eyelids closed.

My senses faded from me one by one;

I knew no more until I found myself,

After a strange dark interval of time,

Once more upon my hated pedestal.

A statue – motionless – insensible.

And then I saw the glorious gods come down!

Down to this room! the air was filled with them!

They came and looked upon Pygmalion,

And looking on him, kissed him one by one,

And said, in tones that spoke to me of life,

'We cannot take her from such happiness!

Live Galatea for his love!' And then

The glorious light that I had lost came back –

There was Myrine's room, there was her couch,

There was the sun in heaven; and the birds

Sang once more in the great green waving trees,

As I had heard them sing – I lived once more

To look on him I love!

from THE CABINET MINISTER

by *Sir Arthur Wing Pinero (1855-1934)*

LADY TWOMBLEY: Dear old Lady Leeke, whose wheels we locked in the Park, said she had heard Imogen's name mentioned fifty times. Mrs Charlie Lessingham declares nothing prettier has been seen since her own first season. And it's true – that's the best of it! I saw the child make her courtesy; I was determined I would. I entered the Throne Room just before her and tumbled through anyhow, with one eye straight in front of me and the other screwed round towards my girl. There was a general shudder – it was at my squint.

[. . .]

When I did get through they gave me my train as much as to say: 'If this belongs to you, take it home as soon as possible.' But there I stuck in the doorway, not budging an inch. I didn't care how the officials whispered, and waved, and beckoned; I stood my ground. And then, Julian, then my breath nearly went from me, for I saw her coming! Effie, it was lovely! Brooke, you would have been proud of your sister! Her cheeks were like the outside leaf of a Duchesse de Vallombrosa rose, and her eyes like two dewdrops on the top of it; and she had just enough fright in her little heart to make her feathers tremble. Then she courtesied. Ah, if she had stumbled I should have been by her side in an instant – who would have blamed me? I'm her mother! – but she didn't. No, she floated towards me – dipping, and dipping, and dipping, again and again, as smoothly and gracefully as a swan swimming backward!

from PAOLO AND FRANCESCA

by *Stephen Phillips (1864-1915)*

LUCREZIA: Spared! to be spared what I was born to have!

        I am a woman, and this very flesh

        Demands its natural pangs, its rightful throes,

        And I implore with vehemence these pains.

        I know that children wound us, and surprise

        Even to utter death, till we at last

        Turn from a face to flowers: but this my heart

        Was ready for these pangs, and had foreseen.

        O! but I grudge the mother her last look

        Upon the coffined form – that pang is rich –

        Envy the shivering cry when gravel falls.

        And all these maimèd wants and thwarted thoughts,

        Eternal yearning, answered by the wind,

        Have dried in me belief and love and fear.

        I am become a danger and a menace,

        A wandering fire, a disappointed force,

        A peril – do you hear, Giovanni? – O!

        It is such souls as mine that go to swell

        The childless cavern cry of the barren sea,

        Or make that human ending to night-wind.

        Why have I bared myself to you? – I know not,

        Unless, indeed, this marriage – yes, this marriage –

        Near now, is't not? – So near made me cry out.

        Ah! she will bring a sound of pattering feet!

        But now this message – and those papers. I

        Must haste to see the banquet-table spread –

        Your bride is yet so young.

from LONDON ASSURANCE

by *Dion Boucicault (1820-1890)*

Enter Meddle, with a newspaper.

MEDDLE: I have secured the only newspaper in the village my character as an attorney-at-law depended on the monopoly of its information. – I took it up by chance when this paragraph met my astonished view: (*Reads*:) "We understand that the contract of marriage so long in abeyance on account of the lady's minority, is about to be celebrated, at Oak Hall, Gloucestershire, the well-known and magnificent mansion of Maximilian Harkaway, Esq., between Sir Harcourt Courtly, Baronet, of fashionable celebrity, and Miss Grace Harkaway, niece to the said Mr Harkaway. The preparations are proceeding on the good old English style.' Is it possible! I seldom swear, except in a witness box, but damme, had it been known in the village, my reputation would have been lost; my voice in the parlour of the Red Lion mute, and Jenks, a fellow who calls himself a lawyer, without more capability than a broomstick, and as much impudence as a young barrister, after getting a verdict, by mistake; why, he would actually have taken the Reverend Mr Spout by the button, which is now my sole privilege. Ah! here is Mrs Pert; couldn't have hit upon a better person. I'll cross-examine her – Lady's maid to Miss Grace, confidential purloiner of second-hand silk – a *nisi prius* of her mistress – Ah! sits on the woolsack in the pantry, and dictates the laws of kitchen etiquette. – Ah! Mrs Pert, good morning; permit me to say, – and my word as a legal character is not unduly considered – I venture to affirm, that you look a – quite like the – a –

ALCM

from JOHN GILPIN

by *William Cowper (1731-1800)*

John Gilpin was a citizen
   Of credit and renown,
A train-band captain eke was he
   Of famous London town.

John Gilpin's spouse said to her dear:
   'Though wedded we have been
These twice ten tedious years, yet we
   No holiday have seen.

'To-morrow is our wedding-day,
   And we will then repair
Unto the Bell at Edmonton,
   All in a chaise and pair.

'My sister, and my sister's child,
   Myself, and children three,
Will fill the chaise; so you must ride
   On horseback after we.'

He soon replied: 'I do admire
   Of womankind but one,
And you are she, my dearest dear,
   Therefore it shall be done.

'I am a linen-draper bold,
   As all the world doth know,
And my good friend the calender
   Will lend his horse to go.'

Quoth Mrs Gilpin: 'That's well said;
   And for that wine is dear,
We will be furnished with our own,
   Which is both bright and clear.'

John Gilpin kissed his loving wife;
   O'erjoyed was he to find,
That though on pleasure she was bent
   She had a frugal mind.

A RECEIPT TO CURE THE VAPOURS

by *Lady Mary Wortley Montagu*
(1689-1762)

Why will Delia thus retire
   And languish Life away?
While the sighing Crowds admire
   'Tis too soon for Hartshorn Tea.

All these dismal looks and fretting
   Cannot Damon's life restore,
Long ago the Worms have eat him,
   You can never see him more.

Once again consult your Toilet,
   In the Glass your Face review,
So much weeping soon will spoil it
   And no Spring your Charms renew.

I like you was born a Woman –
   Well I know what Vapours mean,
The Disease alas! is common,
   Single we have all the Spleen.

All the Morals that they tell us
   Never cur'd Sorrow yet,
Chuse among the pretty Fellows
   One of humour, Youth, and Wit.

Prithee hear him ev'ry Morning
   At least an hour or two,
Once again at Nights returning,
   I beleive the Dose will do.

IS THERE FOR HONEST POVERTY
by *Robert Burns (1759-1796)*

Is there for honest poverty
   That hings his head, an' a' that?
The coward slave, we pass him by –
   We dare be poor for a' that,
      For a' that, an' a' that,
        Our toils obscure, an' a' that,
      The rank is but the guinea's stamp,
      The man's the gowd for a' that.

What tho' on hamely fare we dine,
   Wear hodden grey, an' a' that?
Gie fools their silks, and knaves their wine –
   A man's a man for a' that!
      For a' that, an' a' that,
        Their tinsel show, an' a' that,
      The honest man, tho' e'er sae poor,
      Is king o' men for a' that.

Ye see yon birkie ca'd a lord,
   Wha struts, and stares, an' a' that;
Tho' hundreds worship at his word,
   He's but a coof for a' that.
      For a' that, an' a' that,
        His ribband, star, an' a' that,
      The man o' independent mind,
      He looks an' laughs at a' that.

A prince can mak a belted knight,
   A marquis, duke, an' a' that,
But an honest man's aboon his might –
   Gude faith, he mauna fa' that!
      For a' that, an' a' that,
        Their dignities, an' a' that,
      The pith o' sense an' pride o' worth
      Are higher rank than a' that.

Then let us pray that come it may –
   As come it will, for a' that –
That sense and worth, o'er a' the earth
   Shall bear the gree, an' a' that;
      For a' that, an' a' that,
        It's comin yet for a' that,
      That man to man the world o'er,
      Shall brothers be for a' that.

from AN ESSAY ON MAN
by *Alexander Pope (1688-1744)*

Know then thyself, presume not God to scan;
The proper study of mankind is Man.
Plac'd on this isthmus of a middle state,
A being darkly wise, and rudely great:
With too much knowledge for the sceptic side,
With too much weakness for the stoic's pride,
He hangs between; in doubt to act, or rest;
In doubt to deem himself a god, or beast;
In doubt his mind or body to prefer:
Born but to die, and reas'ning but to err;
Alike in ignorance, his reason such,
Whether he thinks too little, or too much:
Chaos of thought and passion, all confus'd:
Still by himself abus'd, or disabus'd;
Created half to rise, and half to fall;
Great lord of all things, yet a prey to all;
Sole judge of truth, in endless error hurl'd:
The glory, jest, and riddle of the world!

from SIR ROGER AT VAUXHALL

by *Joseph Addison (1672-1719)*

We were no sooner come to the Temple-stairs, but we were surrounded by a crowd of watermen, offering their respective services. Sir Roger, after having looked about him very attentively, spied one with a wooden leg, and immediately gave him orders to get his boat ready. As we were walking towards it, 'You must know (says Sir Roger), I never make use of anybody to row me that has not either lost a leg or an arm. I would rather bate him a few strokes of his oar, than not employ an honest man that has been wounded in the Queen's service. If I was a lord or a bishop, and kept a barge, I would not put a fellow in my livery that had not a wooden leg.'

My old friend, after having seated himself, and trimmed the boat with his coachman, who, being a very sober man, always serves for ballast on these occasions, we made the best of our way for Fox-hall. Sir Roger obliged the waterman to give us the history of his right leg, and hearing that he had left it at La Hogue, with many particulars which passed in that glorious action, the knight in the triumph of his heart made several reflections on the greatness of the British nation; as, that one Englishman could beat three Frenchmen; that we could never be in danger of Popery so long as we took care of our fleet; that the Thames was the noblest river in Europe; that London bridge was a greater piece of work than any other of the seven wonders of the world; with many other honest prejudices which naturally cleave to the heart of a true Englishman.

After some short pause, the old knight, turning about his head twice or thrice to take a survey of this great metropolis, bid me observe how thick the city was set with churches, and that there was scarce a single steeple on this side Temple-bar. 'A most heathenish sight! (says Sir Roger): There is no religion at this end of the town. The fifty new churches will very much mend the prospect; but church-work is slow, church-work is slow!'

from THE WEDDING OF JENNY DISTAFF

by *Richard Steele (1672-1729)*

"This, dear Jenny, is the reason that the quarrel between Sir Harry Willit and his lady, which began about her squirrel, is irreconcilable. Sir Harry was reading a grave author; she runs into his study, and in a playing humour, claps the squirrel upon the folio: he threw the animal in a rage upon the floor; she snatches it up again, calls Sir Harry a sour pedant, without good nature or good manners. This cast him into such a rage, that he threw down the table before him, kicked the book round the room; then recollected himself: 'Lord, madam,' said he, 'why did you run into such expressions? I was,' said he, 'in the highest delight with that author, when you clapped your squirrel upon my book'; and, smiling, added upon recollection, 'I have great respect for your favourite, and pray let us all be friends.' My lady was so far from accepting this apology, that she immediately conceived a resolution to keep him under for ever: and with a serious air replied, 'There is no regard to be had to what a man says, who can fall into so indecent a rage, and such an abject submission, in the same moment, for which I absolutely despise you.' Upon which she rushed out of the room. Sir Harry staid some minutes behind, to think and command himself; after which he followed her into her bed-chamber, where she was prostrate upon the bed, tearing her hair, and naming twenty coxcombs who would have used her otherwise. This provoked him to so high a degree, that he forbore nothing but beating her; and all the servants in their family were at their several stations listening, whilst the best man and woman, the best master and mistress, defamed each other in a way that is not to be repeated even at Billingsgate. You know this ended in an immediate separation: she longs to return home, but knows not how to do it: he invites her home every day. Her husband requires no submission of her; but she thinks her very return will argue she is to blame, which she is resolved to be for ever, rather than acknowledge it. Thus, dear Jenny, my great advice to you is, be guarded against giving or receiving little provocations. Great matters of offence I have not reason to fear either from you or your husband."

from LE FEVRE

by *Laurence Sterne (1713-1768)*

'Stay in the room a little,' said my uncle Toby. 'Trim!' said my uncle Toby, after he had lighted his pipe and smoked about a dozen whiffs. Trim came in front of his master, and made his bow; – my uncle Toby smoked on and said no more. 'Corporal!' said my uncle Toby; the corporal made his bow. My uncle Toby proceeded no farther, but finished his pipe.

'Trim!' said my uncle Toby, 'I have a project in my head, as it is a bad night, of wrapping myself up warm in my roquelaur, and paying a visit to this poor gentleman.' 'Your honour's roquelaur,' replied the corporal, 'has not once been had on, since the night before your honour received your wound, when we mounted guard in the trenches before the gate at St. Nicholas; and besides it is so cold and rainy at night, that what with the roquelaur, and what with the weather, 'twill be enough to give your honour your death, and bring on your honour's torment in your groin.' 'I fear so,' replied my uncle Toby; 'but I am not at rest in my mind, Trim, since the account the landlord has given me. I wish I had not known so much of this affair,' added my uncle Toby, 'or that I had known more of it: how shall we manage it?' 'Leave it, an' please your honour, to me,' quoth the corporal; 'I'll take my hat and stick and go to the house and reconnoitre, and act accordingly; and I will bring your honour a full account in an hour.' 'Thou shalt go, Trim,' said my uncle Toby, 'and here's a shilling for thee to drink with his servant.' 'I shall get it all out of him,' said the corporal, shutting the door.

My uncle Toby filled his second pipe; and had it not been that he now and then wandered from the point, with considering whether it was not full as well to have the curtain of the tenaille a straight line, as a crooked one, he might be said to have thought of nothing else but poor Le Fevre and his boy the whole time he smoked it.

A LETTER TO GEORGE MONTAGU

from *Horace Walpole (1717-1797)*

Strawberry Hill, Oct. 21, 1759.

Your pictures shall be sent as soon as any of us go to London, but I think that will not be till the Parliament meets. Can one easily leave the remains of such a year as this? It is still all gold. I have not dined or gone to bed by a fire till the day before yesterday. Instead of the glorious and ever-memorable year 1759, as the newspapers call it, I call it this ever-warm and victorious year. We have not had more conquest than fine weather: one would think we had plundered East and West Indies of sunshine. Our bells are worn threadbare with ringing for victories. I believe it will require ten votes of the House of Commons before people will believe that it is the Duke of Newcastle that has done all this and not Mr Pitt. One thing is very fatiguing; all the world is made knights or generals. Adieu! I don't know a word of news less than the conquest of America.

Yours ever

H. W.

PS. You shall hear from me again if we take Mexico or China before Christmas.

PPS. I had sealed my letter, but break it open again, having forgot to tell you that Mr Cowslade has the pictures of Lord and Lady Cutts, and is willing to sell them.

from THE FUNERAL

by *Richard Steele (1672-1729)*

WIDOW: That's right. (*reading names*) Lady Riggle, Lady Formal . . . Oh! that Riggle, a pert ogler, an indiscreet silly thing, who is really known by no man, yet for her carriage justly thought common to all; and as Formal has only the appearance of virtue, so she has only the appearance of vice. What chance, I wonder, put these contradictions to each other into the same coach, as you say they called? Mrs. Frances and Mrs. Winifred Glebe – who are they?

[. . .]

Did I say so? Really I think 'twas apt enough, now I remember 'em. Lady Wrinkle . . . oh, that smug old woman! There's no enduring her affectation of youth, but I plague her; I always ask whether her daughter in Wiltshire has a grandchild yet or not. Lady Worthy . . . I can't bear her company, she has so much of that virtue in her heart which I have in my mouth only (*aside*). Mrs. After-Day . . . oh that's she that was the great beauty, the mighty toast about town – that's just come out of the small-pox; she's horribly pitted they say; I long to see her and plague her with my condolence. 'Tis a pure ill-natured satisfaction to see one that was a beauty unfortunately move with the same languor and softness of behaviour that once was charming in her – to see, I say, her mortify that used to kill. Ha! Ha! Ha! The rest are a catalogue of mere names or titles they were born to, an insipid crowd of neither good nor bad; but you are sure these other ladies suspect not in the least that I know of their coming?

from THE HISTORICAL REGISTER FOR THE YEAR 1736

by *Henry Fielding (1707-1754)*

PISTOL: Associates, brethren, countrymen and friends,
Partakers with us in this glorious enterprise,
Which for our consort we have undertaken,
It grieves us much, yes, by the gods it does!
That we whose great ability and parts
Have raised us to this pinnacle of power,
Entitling us Prime Minister theatrical,
That we should with an upstart of the stage
Contend successless on our consort's side.
But though by just hereditary right
We claim a lawless power, yet for some reasons,
Which to ourself we keep as yet concealed,
Thus to the public deign we to appeal.   (*Kneels.*)
Behold how humbly the great Pistol kneels.
Say then, O town, is it your royal will
That my great consort represent the part
Of Polly Peachum in *The Beggar's Opera*?   (*Mob hiss.*)
Thanks to the town – that hiss speaks their assent.
Such was the hiss that spoke the great applause
Our mighty father met with when he brought
His *Riddle* on the stage. Such was the hiss
Welcomed his *Caesar* to the Egyptian shore;
Such was the hiss in which great *John* should have expired.
But wherefore do I try in vain to number
Those glorious hisses which from age to age
Our family has borne triumphant from the stage?

from DISTRESS UPON DISTRESS

by *George Alexander Stevens (1710-1784)*

ARIETTA: I to the Creature send, excuse me Ma'am,

What like a Wife petition? if I do;

And now, I think on't, I will make a Vow.

Hear me ye Naiads, Fairies, Nymphs and Fawns,

Who wanton lave amidst the chrystal Streams;

That o'er the smooth-worn Pebbles plays

Thro' flow'ry Vales, and daisy-sprinkled Meads:

And ye who govern the high-waving Woods;

Who secret dwell in sun-sequestred Groves,

And nightly dance thro' arch-embower'd Walks.

Ye Hamadryads hear! Ye sullen Gnomes

That flit on foggy Clouds from Earth uprais'd:

Ye purer Sylphs, that skim the midway Air;

And all ye Genii of the Deep attend.

If I request, petition, send, or sue,

May Thunder split my Snuff-box all to pieces,

And Lightnings burn my *Brussels* Mob to Ashes.

[. . .]

I'll be blind first truly; no, I'll now,

With weary, wandring, melancholy, tread;

Goaded by Griefs, disconsolately creep:

On the soft Pillow rest my aching Head,

Sob like a Child, and sigh my self to sleep,

Snore out my Wrongs and dream – the Lord knows what.

What I in Vision see, that I'll fullfil,

If 'tis my Blood, or Pen-dipt-Ink to spill:

To end my Woes at once by well-set Knife,

Or vindicate my Wrongs, and write my Life.

Epilogue from POLLY HONEYCOMBE

by *David Garrick (1717-1779)*

POLLY: My poor Papa's in woeful agitation –

While I, the Cause, feel here, (*Striking her bosom*) no palpitation –

We Girls of Reading, and superior notions,

Who from the fountain-head drink love's sweet potions,

Pity our parents, when such passion blinds 'em,

One hears the good folks rave – One never minds 'em.

Till these dear books infus'd their soft ingredients,

Asham'd and fearful, I was all Obedience.

Then my good Father did not storm in vain,

I blush'd and cry'd – *I'll ne'er do so again*:

But now no bugbears can my spirit tame,

I've conquer'd Fear – And almost conquer'd Shame;

So much these Dear Instructors change and win us,

Without their *light* we ne'er should know what's in us:

Here we at once supply our childish wants –

NOVELS are Hotbeds for your forward Plants.

Not only Sentiments refine the Soul,

But hence we learn to be the Smart and Drole;

Each awkward circumstance for laughter serves,

From Nurse's nonsense to my Mother's *NERVES*:

    Tho' Parents tell us, that our genius lies

In mending linnen and in making pies,

I set such formal precepts at defiance

That preach up prudence, neatness, and compliance:

Leap these old bounds, and boldly set the pattern,

To be a Wit, Philosopher, and Slattern –

    O! did all Maids and Wives, my spirit feel,

We'd make this topsy-turvy world to reel:

Let us to arms! – Our Fathers, Husbands, dare!

NOVELS will teach us all the Art of War:

Our Tongues will serve for Trumpet and for Drum;

I'll be your Leader – General *HONEYCOMBE*!

    Too long has human nature gone astray,

Daughters should govern, Parents should obey;

Man shou'd submit, the moment that he weds,

And hearts of oak shou'd yield to wiser heads:

I see you smile bold *Britons*! – But 'tis true –

Beat *You* the *French*; – But let your *Wives* beat *You*. –

from THE GOOD NATUR'D MAN

by *Oliver Goldsmith (c.1730-1774)*

CROAKER: Death and destruction! Are all the horrors of air, fire and water to be levelled only at me! Am I only to be singled out for gun-powder plots, combustibles, and conflagration! Here it is – An incendiary letter dropped at my door. *To Muster Croaker, these, with speed.* Ay, ay, plain enough the direction: all in the genuine incendiary spelling, and as cramp as the devil. *With speed.* Oh, confound your speed. But let me read it once more. (*Reads:*) *Mustar Croaker as sone as yoew see this leve twenty gunnes at the bar of the Talboot tell caled for yowe and yower experetion will be al blown up*! Ah, but too plain! Blood and gunpowder in every line of it. Blown up! murderous dog! All blown up! Heavens! what have I and my poor family done, to be all blown up? (*Reads:*) *Our pockets are low, and money we must have.* Ay, there's the reason; they'll blow us up, because they have got low pockets. (*Reads:*) *It is but a short time you have to consider; for if this takes wind, the house will quickly be all of a flame.* Inhuman monsters! blow us up, and then burn us. The earthquake at Lisbon was but a bonfire to it! (*Reads:*) *Make quick dispatch, and so no more at present. But may Cupid, the little God of Love, go with you wherever you go.* The little God of Love! Cupid, the little God of Love go with me! Go you to the devil, you and your little Cupid together; I'm so frightened, I scarce know whether I sit, stand, or go. Perhaps this moment I'm treading on lighted matches, blazing brimstone and barrels of gunpowder. They are preparing to blow me up into the clouds. Murder! We shall all be burnt in our beds; we shall be all burnt in our beds.

from DOUGLAS

by *John Home (1722-1808)*

NORVAL: Small is the skill my Lord delights to praise
    In him he favours. – Hear from whence it came.
    Beneath a mountain's brow, the most remote
    And inaccessible by shepherds trod,
    In a deep cave, dug by no mortal hand,
    A hermit liv'd; a melancholy man,
    Who was the wonder of our wand'ring swains.
    Austere and lonely, cruel to himself,
    Did they report him; the cold earth his bed,
    Water his drink, his food the shepherd's alms.
    I went to see him, and my heart was touch'd
    With rev'rence and with pity. Mild he spake,
    And, entring on discourse, such stories told
    As made me oft revisit his sad cell.
    For he had been a soldier in his youth;
    And fought in famous battles, when the Peers
    Of Europe, by the bold GODFREDO led,
    Against th'usurping Infidel display'd
    The cross of Christ, and won the Holy Land.
    Pleas'd with my admiration, and the fire
    His speech struck from me, the old man wou'd shake
    His years away, and act his young encounters:
    Then, having shew'd his wounds, he'd sit him down,
    And all the live-long day discourse of war.
    To help my fancy, in the smooth green turf
    He cut the figures of the marshall'd hosts;
    Describ'd the motions, and explain'd the use
    Of the deep column, and the lengthen'd line,
    The square, the crescent, and the phalanx firm.
    For all that Saracen or Christian knew
    Of war's vast art, was to this hermit known.

from THE IRON CHEST

by *George Colman the Younger (1762-1836)*

HELEN: I'll mimick the physician — wise and dull —

With cane at nose, and nod emphatical,

Portentous in my silence; feel your pulse,

With an owl's face, that shall express as much

As Galen's head, cut out in wood, and gilt,

Stuck over an apothecary's door.

[. . .]

I would distil

Each flower that lavish happiness produced,

Through the world's paradise, ere Disobedience

Scatter'd the seeds of care; then mingle each,

In one huge cup of comfort for thee, love,

To chace away thy dulness. Thou shouldst wanton

Upon the wings of Time, and mock his flight,

As he sail'd with thee tow'rd Eternity.

I'd have each hour, each minute of thy life,

A golden holiday; and should a cloud

O'ercast thee, be it light as gossamer,

That Helen might disperse it with her breath,

And talk thee into sunshine!

[. . .]

My Mortimer! You — Oh! for heaven's sake,

Do not talk thus! You chill me. You are well;

Very well. — You give way — Oh, Mortimer!

Banish these fantasies. Think on poor Helen!

Oh! for pity —

[. . .]

What have I done, that you —   (*bursts into tears.*)

[. . .]

I did not mean to weep. Oh, Mortimer,

I could not talk so cruelly to you!

I would not pain you thus, for worlds!

Prologue from THE ROVERS

by *George Canning (1770-1827), John Hookham Frere (1769-1846)*

and George Ellis (1753-1815)

Too long the triumphs of our early times,

With civil discord and with regal crimes,

Have stain'd these boards; while Shakespeare's pen has shewn

Thoughts, manners, men, to modern days unknown.

Too long have Rome and Athens been *the rage*;   (*Applause*)

And classic Buskins soil'd a British Stage.

To-night our Bard, who scorns pedantic rules,

His Plot has borrow'd from the German schools;

– The German schools – where no dull maxims bind

The bold expansion of the electric mind.

Fix'd to no period, circled by no space,

He leaps the flaming bounds of time and place:

Round the dark confines of the forest raves,

With *gentle* Robbers stocks his gloomy caves;

Tells how Prime Ministers are shocking things,

And *reigning Dukes* as bad as tyrant Kings;

How to *two* swains *one* nymph her vows may give,

And how *two* damsels with *one* lover live!

Delicious scenes! – such scenes *our* Bard displays,

Which, crown'd with German, sue for British, praise.

Slow are the steeds, that through Germania's roads

With hempen rein the slumbering post-boy goads;

Slow is the slumbering post-boy, who proceeds

Thro' deep sands floundering, on those tardy steeds;

More slow, more tedious, from his husky throat

Twangs through the twisted horn the struggling note.

These truths confess'd – Oh! yet, ye travell'd few,

Germania's *Plays* with eyes unjaundic'd view!

View and approve! – though in each passage fine

The faint translation mock the genuine line,

Though the nice ear the erring sight belie,

For *U twice dotted* is pronounced like *I*;   (*Applause*)

Yet oft the scene shall nature's fire impart,

Warm *from* the breast, and glowing *to* the heart!

Ye travell'd few, attend! – On *you* our Bard

Builds his fond hope! Do you his genius guard!   (*Applause*)

Nor let succeeding generations say

   – A British Audience *damn'd* a German play!

TO MEADOWS
by *Robert Herrick (1591-1674)*

Ye have been fresh and green,
　　Ye have been filled with flowers:
And ye the walks have been
　　Where maids have spent their hours.

You have beheld, how they
　　With wicker arks did come
To kiss, and bear away
　　The richer cowslips home.

You've heard them sweetly sing,
　　And seen them in a round:
Each virgin, like a spring,
　　With honey-suckles crowned.

But now we see none here,
　　Whose silvery feet did tread,
And with dishevelled hair,
　　Adorned this smoother mead.

Like unthrifts, having spent
　　Your stock, and needy grown,
You're left here to lament
　　Your poor estates, alone.

LOVE
by *George Herbert (1593-1633)*

Love bade me welcome: yet my soul drew back,
　　　　　Guilty of dust and sin.
But quick-eyed Love, observing me grow slack
　　　　　From my first entrance in,
Drew nearer to me, sweetly questioning,
　　　　　If I lacked any thing.

'A guest,' I answered, 'worthy to be here.'
　　　　　Love said, 'You shall be he.'
'I, the unkind, ungrateful? Ah! my dear,
　　　　　I cannot look on thee.'
Love took my hand, and smiling did reply,
　　　　　'Who made the eyes but I?'

'Truth, Lord! but I have marred them: let my shame
　　　　　Go where it doth deserve.'
'And know you not,' says Love, 'who bore the blame?'
　　　　　'My dear, then I will serve.'
'You must sit down,' says Love, 'and taste my meat.'
　　　　　So I did sit and eat.

OF THE LAST VERSES IN THE BOOK
by *Edmund Waller (1606-1687)*

When we for age could neither read nor write,
The subject made us able to indite.
The soul with nobler resolutions decked,
The body stooping, does herself erect:
No mortal parts are requisite to raise
Her that unbodied can her Maker praise.

The seas are quiet, when the winds give o'er;
So calm are we, when passions are no more:
For then we know how vain it was to boast
Of fleeting things, so certain to be lost.
Clouds of affection from our younger eyes
Conceal that emptiness, which age descries.

The soul's dark cottage, battered and decayed,
Lets in new light through chinks that time has made.
Stronger by weakness, wiser, men become
As they draw near to their eternal home:
Leaving the old, both worlds at once they view
That stand upon the threshold of the new.

LONG BETWIXT LOVE AND FEAR
by *John Dryden (1631-1700)*

Long betwixt love and fear, Phyllis, tormented,
Shunned her own wish, yet at last she consented:
But loth that day should her blushes discover,
　　'Come, gentle Night,' she said,
　　'Come quickly to my aid,
　　And a poor shame-faced maid
　　　　Hide from her lover.

'Now cold as ice I am, now hot as fire,
I dare not tell myself my own desire;
But let day fly away, and let night haste her:
　　Grant, ye kind Powers above,
　　Slow hours to parting love;
　　But when to bliss we move,
　　　　Bid 'em fly faster.

'How sweet it is to love when I discover
That fire which burns my heart, warming my lover;
'Tis pity love so true should be mistaken:
　　But if this night he be
　　False or unkind to me,
　　Let me die ere I see
　　　　That I'm forsaken.'

from ON DREAMS

by *Sir Thomas Browne (1605-1682)*

Half our days we pass in the shadow of the earth; and the brother of death exacteth a third part of our lives. A good part of our sleep is peered out with visions and fantastical objects, wherein we are confessedly deceived. The day supplieth us with truths; the night with fictions and falsehoods, which uncomfortably divide the natural account of our beings. And, therefore, having passed the day in sober labours and rational enquiries of truth, we are fain to betake ourselves unto such a state of being, wherein the soberest heads have acted all the monstrosities of melancholy, and which unto open eyes are no better than folly and madness.

Happy are they that go to bed with grand music, like Pythagoras, or have ways to compose the fantastical spirit, whose unruly wanderings take off inward sleep, filling our heads with St Anthony's visions, and the dreams of Lipara in the sober chambers of rest.

Virtuous thoughts of the day lay up good treasures for the night; whereby the impressions of imaginary forms arise into sober similitudes, acceptable unto our slumbering selves and preparatory unto divine impressions. Hereby Solomon's sleep was happy. Thus prepared, Jacob might well dream of angels upon a pillow of stone. And the best sleep of Adam might be the best of any after.

That there should be divine dreams seems unreasonably doubted by Aristotle. That there are demoniacal dreams we have little reason to doubt. Why may there not be angelical? If there be guardian spirits, they may not be inactively about us in sleep; but may sometimes order our dreams: and many strange hints, instigations, or discourses, which are so amazing unto us, may arise from such foundations.

A LETTER TO LAURENCE HYDE

from *Elinor (Nell) Gwyn (1650-1687)*

1682

pray Deare Mr. Hide forgive me for not writeing to you before now for the reasone is I have bin sick thre months & sinse I recovered I have had nothing to intertaine you withall nor have nothing now worth writing but that I can holde no longer to let you know I never have ben in any companie wethout drinking your health. for I love you with all my soule. the pel mel is now to me a dismale plase sinse I have uterly lost Sir Car Scrope never to be recovred agane for he tould me he could not live allwayes at this rate & so begune to be a littel uncivil, which I could not sufer from an uglye *baux garscon*. Ms Knights Lady mothers dead & she has put up a scrutchin no beiger than my Lady grins scunchis. My lord Rochester is gon in the cuntrei. Mr Savil has got a misfortune, but is upon recovery & is to mary an hairres, who I thinke wont wont have an ill time ont if he holds up his thumb. My lord of Dorscit apiers wonse in thre munths, for he drinkes aile with Shadwell & Mr Haris at the Dukes house all day long. my Lord Burford remimbers his sarvis to you. my Lord Bauclaire isis goeing into france. we are a goeing to supe with the king at whithall & my lady Harvie. the King remembers his sarvis to you. now lets talke of state affairs, for we never caried things so cunningly as now for we dont know whether we shall have pesce or war, but I am for war and for no other reason but that you may come home. I have a thousand merry conseets, but I cant make her write um & therfore you must take the will for the deed. god bye. your most loveing obedunt faithfull & humbel sarvant

E.G.

from his DIARY

by *John Evelyn (1620-1706)*

23rd May, 1652

The morning growing excessively hot, I sent my footman some hours before, and so rod negligently, under favour of the shade, 'til being now come to within three miles of Bromley, at a place called the procession Oake, started out two Cutt-throates, and striking with their long staves at the horse, taking hold of the reignes, threw me downe, and immediately tooke my sword, and haled me into a deepe Thickett, some quarter of a mile from the high-way, where they might securely rob me, as they soone did; what they got of mony was not considerable, but they tooke two rings, the one an emrald with diamonds, an Onyx, and a pair of boucles set with rubies and diamonds which were of value, and after all, barbarously bound my hands behind me, and my feete, having before pull'd off my bootes: and then set up against an Oake, with most bloudy threatnings to cutt my throat, if I offred to crie out, or make any noise, for that they should be within hearing, I not being the person they looked for: I told them, if they had not basely surpriz'd me, they should not have made so easy a prize, and that it should teach me hereafter never to ride neere an hedge; since had I ben in the mid way, they durst not have adventur'd on me, at which they cock'd their pistols, and told me they had long guns too, and were 14 companions, which all were lies: I begg'd for my Onyx and told them it being engraven with my armes, would betray them, but nothing prevaild: My horse bridle they slipt, and search'd the saddle which they likewise pull'd off, but let the horse alone to graze, and then turning againe bridld him, and tied him to a Tree, yet so as he might graze, and so left so bound: The reason they tooke not my horse, was I suppose, because he was mark'd, and cropt on both Eares, and well known on that roade, and these rogues were lusty foote padders, as they are cald: Well, being left in this manner, grievously was I tormented with the flies, the ants, and the sunn, so as I sweate intollerably, nor little was my anxiety how I should get loose in that solitary place, where I could neither heare or see any creature but my poore horse and a few sheepe stragling in the Coppse; til after neere two houres attempting I got my hands to turne paulme to paulme, whereas before they were tied back to back, and then I stuck a greate while ere' I could slip the cord over my wrist to my thumb, which at last I did, and then being quite loose soone unbound my feete, and so sadling my horse, and roaming a while about, I at last perceiv'd a dust to rise, and soone after heard the rattling of a Cart, towards which I made, and by the help of two Country fellows that were driving it, got downe a steepe bank, into the highway againe; but could heare nothing of the Villians: So I rod to Colonel Blounts a greate justiciarie of the times, who sent out hugh and Crie immediately.

from THE PILGRIM'S PROGRESS

by *John Bunyan (1628-1688)*

Christian. Pray sir, what may I call you? said Christian.

By-ends. I am a stranger to you, and you to me; if you be going this way, I shall be glad of your company; if not, I must be content.

Christian. This town of Fair-speech, said Christian, I have heard of it, and, as I remember, they say it's a wealthy place.

By-ends. Yes, I will assure you that it is, and I have very many rich kindred there.

Christian. Pray who are your kindred there, if a man may be so bold?

By-ends. Almost the whole town; and in particular, my Lord Turn-about, my Lord Time-server, my Lord Fair-speech (from whose ancestors that town first took its name), also Mr Smooth-man, Mr Facing-bothways, Mr Any-thing, and the parson of our parish, Mr Two-tongues, was my mother's own brother by father's side: and to tell you the truth, I am become a gentleman of good quality; yet my great-grandfather was but a waterman, looking one way and rowing another: and I got most of my estate by the same occupation.

Christian. Are you a married man?

By-ends. Yes, and my wife is a very virtuous woman, the daughter of a virtuous woman. She was my Lady Faining's daughter, therefore she came of a very honourable family, and is arrived to such a pitch of breeding that she knows how to carry it to all, even to prince and peasant. 'Tis true, we somewhat differ in religion from those of the stricter sort, yet but in two small points: first, we never strive against wind and tide; secondly, we are always most zealous when religion goes in his silver slippers; we love much to walk with him in the street if the sun shines and the people applaud it.

from AURENG-ZEBE

by *John Dryden (1631-1700)*

NOURMAHAL: My Thoughts no other Joys but Pow'r pursue:

Or, if they did, they must be lost in you.

And yet the Fault's not mine –

Tho' Youth and Beauty cannot Warmth command;

The Sun in vain shines on the barren Sand.

[. . .]

What's Love to you?

The Bloom of Beauty other Years demands;

Nor will be gather'd by such wither'd Hands:

You importune it with a false Desire:

Which sparkles out, and makes no solid Fire.

This Impudence of Age, whence can it spring?

All you expect, and yet you nothing bring.

Eager to ask, when you are past a Grant;

Nice in providing what you cannot want.

Have Conscience; give not her you love this Pain:

Sollicit not yourself, and her, in vain.

All other Debts may Compensation find:

But Love is strict, and will be paid in kind.

[. . .]

What you merit, have:

And share, at least, the Miseries you gave.

Your Days I will alarm, I'll haunt your Nights:

And, worse than Age, disable your Delights.

May your sick Fame still languish, 'till it die:

All Offices of Pow'r neglected lie,

And you grow cheap in every Subject's Eye.

Then, as the greatest Curse that I can give;

Unpity'd be depos'd; and after live.

from A GAME AT CHESS

by *Thomas Middleton (c.1580-1627)*

FAT BISHOP: 'T is a most lordly life to rail at ease,

Sit, eat, and feed upon the fat of one kingdom,

And rail upon another with the juice on 't.

I have writ this book out of the strength and marrow

Of six and thirty dishes at a meal,

But most on 't out of cullis of cock-sparrows;

'T will stick and glue the faster to the adversary,

'T will slit the throat of their most calvish cause,

And yet I eat but little butcher's meat

In the conception.

Of all things I commend the White House best

For plenty and variety of victuals.

When I was one of the Black side professed

My flesh fell half a cubit, time to turn

When my own ribs revolted. But to say true

I have no preferment yet that's suitable

To the greatness of my person and my parts;

I grant I live at ease, for I am made

The master of the beds, the long-acre of beds,

But there's no marigolds that shuts and opens,

Flower-gentles, Venus-baths, apples of love,

Pinks, hyacinths, honeysuckles, daffadowndillies.

There was a time I had more such drabs than beds,

Now I've more beds than drabs;

Yet there's no eminent trader deals in wholesale

But she and I have clapped a bargain up,

Let in at Watergate, for which I have racked

My tenants' purse-strings that they have twanged again.

[*Enter* BLACK KNIGHT *and* BLACK BISHOP]

Yonder Black Knight, the fistula of Europe,

Whose disease once I undertook to cure

With a High Holborn halter – when he last

Vouchsafed to peep into my privileged lodgings

He saw good store of plate there, and rich hangings;

He knew I brought none to the White House with me.

I have not lost the use of my profession

Since I turned White House Bishop.

from THE ROVER

by *Aphra Behn (1640-1689)*

HELLENA: So, so, now you are provided for there's no care taken of poor me. But since you have set my heart a-wishing, I am resolved to know for what; I will not die of the pip, so I will not.

I don't intend every he that likes me shall have me, but he that I like. I should have stayed in the nunnery still if I had liked my lady abbess as well as she liked me. No, I came thence not, as my wise brother imagines, to take an eternal farewell of the world, but to love and to be beloved; and I will be beloved, or I'll get one of your men, so I will.

Hang your considering lover! I never thought beyond the fancy that 'twas a very pretty, idle, silly kind of pleasure to pass one's time with: to write little soft nonsensical billets, and with great difficulty and danger receive answers in which I shall have my beauty praised, my wit admired, though little or none, and have the vanity and power to know I am desirable. Then I have the more inclination that way because I am to be a nun, and so shall not be suspected to have any such earthly thoughts about me; but when I walk thus – and sigh thus – they'll think my mind's upon my monastery, and cry, 'How happy 'tis she's so resolved.' But not a word of man.

I'll warrant, if my brother hears either of you sigh, he cries gravely, 'I fear you have the indiscretion to be in love, but take heed of the honor of our house, and your own unspotted fame'; and so he conjures on till he has laid the soft winged god in your hearts, or broke the bird's nest. But see, here comes your lover, but where's my inconstant? Let's step aside, and we may learn something.

from THE WEDDING

by *James Shirley (1596-1666)*

BELFARE: Keep me not from him, Captain; he has in this
　　　　　Given a fresh wound. I came t'expostulate
　　　　　The reason of a former suffering,
　　　　　Which unto this was charity. As thou art
　　　　　A gentleman, I dare thee to the combat.
　　　　　Contemn not, Beauford, my grey hairs. If thou'st
　　　　　A noble soul, keep not this distance. Meet me;
　　　　　Thou art a soldier. For heaven's sake permit me
　　　　　Chastise the most uncharitable slander
　　　　　Of this bad man.

　　　　　[Beauford: I never injur'd you.]

　　　　　Not injur'd me? What is there then in nature
　　　　　Left to be call'd an injury? Didst not mock
　　　　　Me, and my poor fond girl, with marriage,
　　　　　Till all things were design'd, the very day
　　　　　When Hymen should have worn his saffron robe,
　　　　　My friends invited, and prepar'd to call
　　　　　Her bride? And yet, as if all this could not,
　　　　　Summ'd up together, make an injury,
　　　　　Does thy corrupted soul at last conspire
　　　　　To take her white name from her? Give me leave
　　　　　To express a father in a tear, or two,
　　　　　For my wrong'd child. O Beauford, thou hast robb'd
　　　　　A father and a daughter. But I will not
　　　　　Usurp heaven's justice, which shall punish thee
　　　　　'Bove my weak arm. May'st thou live to have
　　　　　Thy heart as ill rewarded, to be father
　　　　　At my years, have one daughter and no more,
　　　　　Belov'd as mine, so mock'd, and then call'd whore.

from THE ANTIPODES
by *Richard Brome (c.1590-1652)*

DIANA: My Lord, you may

    Gloze o'er and gild the vice, which you call pleasure,

    With god-like attributes, when it is, at best,

    A sensuality, so far below

    Dishonourable that it is mere beastly,

    Which reason ought to abhor; and I detest it

    More than your former hated offers.

    [. . .]

    Hold, stay there.

    Now should you utter volumes of persuasions,

    Lay the whole world of riches, pleasures, honours

    Before me in full grant, that one last word,

    Husband, and from your own mouth spoke, confutes

    And vilifies even all. The very name

    Of husband, rightly weigh'd and well remember'd,

    Without more law or discipline, is enough

    To govern womankind in due obedience,

    Master all loose affections, and remove

    Those idols which, too much, too many love,

    And you have set before me, to beguile

    Me of the faith I owe him. But, remember

    You grant I have a husband; urge no more.

    I seek his love; 'tis fit he loves no whore.

    [. . .]

    Are you a lord?

    Dare you boast honour and be so ignoble?

    Did not you warrant me upon that pawn

    (Which can take up no money), your blank honour,

    That you would cure his jealousy, which affects him

    Like a sharp sore, if I, to ripen it,

    Would set that counterfeit face of scorn upon him,

    Only in show of disobedience; which

    You won me to, upon your protestation

    To render me unstain'd to his opinion,

    And quit me of his jealousy for ever?

from THE PARSON'S WEDDING

by *Thomas Killigrew (1612-1683)*

CAPTAIN:　　All, all. Some of the company are below already. I have so blown it about. One porter is gone to the Exchange to invite Master Wild's merchant to his wedding, and by the way to bid two or three fruiterers to send in fruit for such a wedding; another in my lady's name to Sall's, for sweet-meats. I swore at Bradborn in his shop myself that I wondered he would disappoint Master Wild for his points, and having so long warning. He protested 'twas not his fault but they were ready and he would send John with them presently. One of the watermen is gone to the melon garden, the other to Cook's at the Bear for some bottles of his best wine, and thence to Gracious Street to the poulterers, and all with directions to send in provisions for Master Wild's wedding. And who should I meet at door but Apricock Tom and Mary, waiting to speak with her young master. They came to beg that they might serve the feast. I promised them they should if they would cry it up and down the town, to bring company, for Master Wild was resolved to keep open house.

But who should I meet at the corner of the Piazza but Joseph Taylor? He tells me there's a new play at the Friars today and I have bespoke a box for Master Wild and his bride.

from THE WAY OF THE WORLD

by *William Congreve (1670-1729)*

LADY WISHFORT:　　Why, if she should be innocent, if she should be wronged after all, ha? I don't know what to think, – and I promise you, her education has been unexceptionable – I may say it; for I chiefly made it my own care to initiate her very infancy in the rudiments of virtue, and to impress upon her tender years a young odium and aversion to the very sight of men. – ay friend, she would have shrieked if she had but seen a man, till she was in her teens. As I'm a person 'tis true – she was never suffered to play with a male child, though but in coats; nay, her very babies were of the feminine gender – O, she never looked a man in the face but her own father, or the chaplain, and him we made a shift to put upon her for a woman, by the help of his long garments, and his sleek face; till she was going in her fifteen.

I warrant you, or she would never have borne to have been catechised by him; and have heard his long lectures against singing and dancing, and such debaucheries; and going to filthy plays; and profane music-meetings, where the lewd trebles squeak nothing but bawdy, and the basses roar blasphemy. O, she would have swooned at the sight or name of an obscene play book – and can I think after all this, that my daughter can be naught? What, a whore? And thought it excommunication to set her foot within the door of a playhouse. O dear friend, I can't believe it, no, no; as she says, let him prove it, let him prove it.

from THE RELAPSE

by *Sir John Vanbrugh (1664-1726)*

LOVELESS: Sure fate has yet some business to be done,

Before Amanda's heart and mine must rest;

Else, why amongst those legions of her sex,

Which throng the world,

Shou'd she pick out for her companion

The only one on earth

Whom nature has endow'd for her undoing?

Undoing was't, I said – Who shall undo her?

Is not her empire fix'd? Am I not hers?

Did she not rescue me, a groveling slave,

When, chain'd and bound by that black tyrant Vice,

I labour'd in his vilest drudgery?

Did she not ransom me, and set me free?

Nay, more:

When by my follies sunk

To a poor tatter'd, despicable beggar,

Did she not lift me up to envy'd fortune?

Give me herself, and all that she possest?

Without a thought of more return,

Than what a poor repenting heart might make her,

Han't she done this? And if she has,

Am I not strongly bound to love her for it?

To love her – Why, do I not love her then?

By earth and heaven, I do!

Nay, I have demonstration that I do:

For I would sacrifice my life to serve her.

Yet hold – If laying down my life

Be demonstration of my love,

What is't I feel in favour of Berinthia?

Acknowledgements

We are grateful to the following parties for granting permission to reprint copyright material in this anthology. Although every effort has been made to contact the owners of the copyright in poems and extracts published here, a few have been impossible to trace. We apologise to anyone whom our enquiries have failed to reach and invite them to contact LCM Examinations for acknowledgement.

Ackroyd, Peter: 'All these...' from *The Diversions of Purley and other Poems* by Peter Ackroyd (Copyright © Peter Ackroyd, 1987) is reproduced by permission of Sheil Land Associates Ltd on behalf of Peter Ackroyd; **Ayckbourn, Alan:** from *Absurd Person Singular* by Alan Ayckbourn, published by Chatto and Windus. Reprinted by permission of The Random House Group Ltd; **Bennett, Alan:** 'A Chip in the Sugar' from *Talking Heads* by Alan Bennett (Copyright © Forelake Ltd 1988) is reproduced by permission of PFD (www.pfd.co.uk) on behalf of Forelake Ltd.; **Blyton, Enid:** *Five Go To Smuggler's Top* written by Enid Blyton and reproduced with the kind permission of Enid Blyton Limited. *Five Go To Smuggler's Top* – Copyright © 1945 Enid Blyton Limited, a Chorion company. All rights reserved; **Bond, Michael:** Excerpt from 'Paddington Goes Underground', from *A Bear Called Paddington* by Michael Bond. Copyright © 1958, renewed 1986 by Michael Bond. Reprinted by permission of Houghton Mifflin Company. All rights reserved; **Brownjohn, Alan:** 'Chameleon' © Alan Brownjohn, 1970; **Clark, Leonard:** 'Which' from *Good Company*, reprinted by permission from The Literary Executor of Leonard Clark; **Cook, Stanley:** 'The Convertibles', 'The Mole', 'The Performing Bag', 'The Stopper' first published by Arc Publications; **Cope, Wendy:** 'Engineers' Corner' from *Making Cocoa for Kingsley Amis*, reproduced by permission of Faber & Faber Ltd.; **Crichton Smith, Iain:** 'The Sea' reprinted by permission of Carcanet Press Ltd.; **Crompton, Richmal:** extract from *William and the Pop Singers* reprinted by permission of A P Watt Ltd on behalf of the Executors of the Estate of Mrs R. C. L. Ashbee; **Dahl, Roald:** extracts from *The Witches*, *The BFG* and *George's Marvellous Medicine* (Jonathan Cape Ltd. and Penguin Books Ltd.) reprinted by permission of David Higham Associates; **De la Mare, Walter:** 'Away Go We', 'High' and 'Silver' reproduced by permission of The Literary Trustees of Walter de la Mare and The Society of Authors as their representative; **Dunstan, Peggy:** 'Mosquito' from *In and Out the Windows* reproduced by permission of Hodder and Stoughton Limited; **Edwards, Richard:** 'The Man Outside' from *Whispers from a Wardrobe*, reprinted by permission of Lutterworth Press; **Fanthorpe, U. A.:** 'Atlas' from *Collected Poems 1978-2003* reproduced by permission of Peterloo Poets; **Friel, Brian:** extracts from *Philadelphia, Here I Come!* and *The Aristocrats* reproduced by permission of Faber & Faber Ltd. and The Catholic University of America Press, Washington DC; **Fry, Christopher:** extract from *A Phoenix Too Frequent* by Christopher Fry (1946) by permission of Oxford University Press; **Fuller, Roy:** 'Snow' and 'Christmas Day' by permission of the copyright holder John Fuller; **Gow, Ronald:** extract from *A Boston Story* first published in 1969 by Josef Weinberger Ltd (pka English Theatre Guild Ltd.). Copyright © 1969 by Ronald Gow. Reprinted by permission of Josef Weinberger Ltd. Applications for performances including staged readings (but excluding examination performances) should be addressed to Josef Weinberger Ltd., 12-14 Mortimer Street, London W1T 3JJ; **Granville Barker, Harley:** extract from *The Voysey Inheritance* reproduced by permission of The Society of Authors as the Literary Representative of the Estate of Harley Granville Barker; **Graves, Robert:** extract from *I, Claudius and Claudius the God*, reprinted by permission of Carcanet Press Ltd.; **Hawcroft, Tricia:** 'The Weed', 'My Pet Mouse', 'The Teddy Bear', 'School' printed with the permission of the author; **Heaney, Seamus:** 'Thatcher' from *Door into the Dark* reproduced by permission of Faber & Faber Ltd.; **Kavanagh, Patrick:** 'Lines Written on a Seat on the Grand Canal, Dublin' is reprinted from *Collected Poems*, edited by Antoinette Quinn (Allen Lane, 2004), by kind permission of the Trustees of the Estate of the late Katherine B. Kavanagh, through the Jonathan Williams Literary Agency; **Kirkup, James:** 'The Broken Toys', 'The Lonely Scarecrow', 'For Old Times' Sake: A Tree Speaks' reprinted by permission of the author; **Kitching, John:** 'Slugs', 'Bored', 'Not Guilty', 'Blue Monday', 'March Snow' reprinted by permission of Trevor Dickinson; **Landesman, Fran:** 'After We've Gone' from *Ballad of the Sad Young Men and Other Verse* reproduced by permission of The Permanent Press Publishing Co.; **Larkin, Philip:** 'The Trees' from *High Windows* reproduced by permission of Faber & Faber Ltd.; **Lewis, C. S.:** *The Last Battle* by C. S. Lewis Pte.

Index of Authors

Index of Titles